er

Rabbits

How to Take Care of Them and Understand Them

With color photographs by Monika Wegler
and Drawings by György Jankovics

Consulting Editor: Lucia Vriends-Parent

BARRON'S

Contents

Preface

There is no cuter sight than a little rabbit squatting on the floor, its nose permanently aquiver and its long ears moving slightly, alert to any sound. If it comes hopping up to us and sits up on its haunches, if it lets itself be petted patiently, or if it starts racing zigzag courses through the room, we feel an acute pleasure. But rabbits display this combination of gentleness and high spirits only if they are cared for properly and kept under conditions that don't violate their basic needs.

What is meant by proper care and conditions is explained in this new pet owner's guide by Monika Wegler, an expert on pet rabbits. She tells which breeds are suitable for an apartment, what you should watch for when buying a cage and accessories, how a rabbit can be housebroken, how to feed the animal properly, and what to do if your rabbit should get sick. All the instructions given are easy to follow so that children, too, can quickly learn what rabbits are like and how to take care of them. Charming color photographs taken by the author—who owns two dwarf rabbits—and many informative drawings by Gyorgy Jankovics convey a lifelike picture of this popular pet, which has been so successful at winning the hearts of children and adults alike.

The author of this book and the editors of Barron's series of pet handbooks wish you much pleasure with your rabbit.

Patient, gentle, and quiet, yet full of energy and courage—this is what your pet rabbit will be like if, by providing proper living conditions and care, you allow it to act out its rabbit nature.

Please read the Note of Warning on page 63.

Advice for Purchase

Rabbits are social animals that languish if they have to be alone too much. If you don't have much free time or if you work away from home all day, you should plan to get two rabbits. Two does will get along especially well if they grow up together.

For most people the word "rabbit," or "bunny," conjures up the image of a cute, cuddly little animal with gentle eyes and a nose that is constantly in motion. And the only commonly known fact about rabbits is that they reproduce at an amazing rate, as in the phrase "multiply like rabbits." This proverbial fertility, by the way, is revered by many cultures, whereas we combat it like the plague. At Easter, we buy and eat chocolate bunnies. We may also think of rabbits as cowards that always run when confronted with danger.

None of these superficial associations does justice to the animal, which is generally underestimated. Did you know, for instance, that rabbits are one of the most popular and widely bred domestic animals and that there are about 50 recognized breeds and varieties of them, including all kinds of colors, sizes and different ear lengths and fur textures? You would also be amazed to see what happens when such a highly bred rabbit manages to escape from its pen and join a nearby colony of wild rabbits. Our tame rabbit slips back into the ways of the wild in no time, and within two generations it will have reverted to the agile, inconspicuously gray shape of its ancestors—a process that is inconceivable in any of our other pets. Can you imagine a carefully manicured lap dog that could transform itself back into a gray wolf hunting through the wild forests?

These are just some of the many things there are to admire about rabbits. Consider also their cheerful nature and sociability, their combination of gentleness and courage, their amazing adaptability, and their nonviolent ways, which are often misinterpreted as arising solely from fear.

Which Rabbit Is Right for You?

Theoretically, all of the many rabbit breeds and mongrels are suitable as a pet. To be sure, a giant rabbit weighing 15 pounds (6.8 kg) or more and measuring up to 28 inches (70 cm) in length is too large to fit in a conventional cage for pets. Even medium-sized breeds are not altogether suitable for being kept exclusively indoors. But here are some examples of rabbits that I can wholeheartedly recommend as pets:

Dwarf rabbits: These weigh no more than 3$\frac{1}{4}$ pounds (1.5 kg), are lively, are bred in many colors, and are especially popular with children because of their round faces and their tiny, cute ears.

Dwarf mongrels: They are usually somewhat larger than their purebred cousins, but they are just as lively and cute and are easier to find because pet stores carry them more commonly.

Small breeds: There are over 20 breeds in this class. They weigh from 5 to 7 pounds (2.25–3.25 kg) and vary greatly in temperament.

Angora: Angoras weigh between 5$\frac{1}{2}$ and 10 pounds (2.5–4.5 kg), are gentle and quiet and therefore ideal for children. They also produce valuable wool, but must be carefully shorn every three months and kept on a wire floor so that their fur does not get fouled or matted.

Fox rabbits: These weigh 5$\frac{1}{2}$ to 8$\frac{3}{4}$ pounds (2.5–4 kg) and are long-haired but don't need to be shorn. Regular brushing is all the coat care that is required.

My dwarf rabbit simply can't resist parsley and broccoli leaves.

Note: Some people have an allergic reaction to rabbit hair. If you think you might be allergic, check with your doctor before getting a rabbit.

Rabbits and Other Pets

Rabbits are sometimes introduced into homes where there are other pets. Many people's love for animals extends beyond any one species, but the desire to have more than one kind of pet can create problems that should be given careful consideration before you buy a rabbit.

Rabbits and guinea pigs: These two animals get along well and can be kept in the same indoor cage, especially if they grow up together.

Birds: Birds that sing loudly or screech should not have their cage in the same room with a rabbit.

Dogs and cats: These animals first have to be taught how to behave with a rabbit, and teaching them is successful only within limits, especially if a dog or cat has been your only pet and is used to being the focus of everyone's attention. In such a situation, jealousy and a hunting instinct that has not previously manifested itself may suddenly erupt. (Take note of the plan for acquainting a rabbit with other pets, page 18.) If the antipathy between the two animals is too great, you should either give up the idea of having a rabbit or accept that the two animals will always have to be kept separate. In my experience, however, the latter alternative does not work if interior space is limited and there are children. Four years ago, Naughty, a 10-week-old tomcat, joined our household, which already included three rabbits. Full of optimism and equipped with well-meant advice from all quarters, I started the acclimation period telling myself, "Any young creature can adapt." But unfortunately things did not work out that way. Naughty kept wrestling with my dwarf doe Mümmi so persistently

In males (above), the genital opening is round and flanked by the testes; the genital opening of the female (below) is slit-like.

that I had to give the cat away. This made all of us very sad, and the fact that we found a good home for him gave us only small comfort.

What Animals Get Along with Each Other?

All rabbits are gregarious and love living together with others of their kind. So if you want to do your rabbit a favor, get it a companion from the very start. Starting out with two rabbits is an especially good idea if you don't have much time and are away from home a lot. Anyone who wants to keep more than two rabbits needs a very large indoor cage or pen.

Two bucks (males) get along peacefully only for the first few months. Once they reach sexual maturity (after about four months) they begin to engage in violent fights for dominance, which can lead to serious injuries.

Two does (females) get along especially well if they grow up together. Two siblings from the same litter will live together most harmoniously.

A pair of rabbits will keep producing offspring, which is not necessarily appreciated by the average pet owner. The best combination, even if you buy the second animal after the first is already established, is to get a female and a castrated male.

Male or Female?

For keeping indoors, a female pet rabbit is preferable. Males have to be castrated because they get very restless otherwise and start spraying urine. This spray has a penetrating sweetish smell that is hard to get rid of.

Determining the sex: Sexing a baby rabbit is not all that easy, and you are best off asking the breeder or a pet dealer who is familiar with rabbits to do it for you. If you want to find out whether an older rabbit is a male, you push down lightly with two fingers on the lower abdomen, carefully stretching the skin until the penis becomes visible. Another unmistakable sign of a male are the testes on each side of the sexual opening, but in a young male they are not yet fully formed.

Dwarf Rabbit or Mongrel?

All baby rabbits are cute and little. But only purebred or pedigreed dwarf rabbits stay little even when fully grown—which is what makes them so popular. With a mongrel or crossbred rabbit from an unknown source, you never know for sure just how it will turn out. Many an unsuspecting pet lover has bought a baby bunny described as a dwarf rabbit only to find some months later that the animal has turned into a regular meat rabbit and is quickly outgrowing the cage originally bought for it. As a matter of fact, the differences that distinguish a purebred dwarf rabbit from a mongrel are quite apparent even in young bunnies (see drawing, page 15). If you don't want to take any chances, your best bet is to buy your dwarf rabbit from a recognized breeder.

Pets as Presents for Children

It seems as though people never spend money as spontaneously and as rashly as when they buy pets for their children. Nobody thinks of the fact that animals are not disposable merchandise that can simply be gotten rid of when their novelty wears off. Yet a school-age child who is thrilled to have a pet today may prefer to spend time playing sports or going to the disco in a few years. The rabbit in the meantime is left in its cage, lonely and sad, if it hasn't been taken to the animal shelter or abandoned long ago. It doesn't have to be this way; everything depends on how the parents teach their children.

Crucial considerations before you buy your child a pet rabbit:
- Arrange to borrow a rabbit for a trial period, perhaps from one of your child's classmates or from some acquaintance. Let your child see what daily life with an animal is like for at least a week, experiencing all the wonderful moments

If you place the rabbit on your lap like this, you will be able to see the genital opening and the anus.

and finding out what owning a rabbit entails, including chores.
- Don't give a rabbit to a child of preschool age.
- Never assume that your child will take on all responsibility for the animal. If you don't want to have anything to do with the rabbit and if you won't enjoy it, you should not get one.
- Try to find out why your child is suddenly asking for a bunny rabbit. Is it just a passing fancy, a wish for something soft and to pet, or is your child perhaps feeling lonely? On the other hand, your child may be motivated by a genuine love for and interest in animals.

Using the tongue to lick the belly.

Using the paws to "wash" the face.

In the photos:
Grooming at the early age of three weeks. Rabbits are among the cleanest of animals. They lick themselves even more than cats do!

My tip: Start out by giving your child a gift certificate. Just about any pet store will be happy to make one out, and you will gain time to think the matter over a little bit more.

Where You Can Get a Pet Rabbit
From pet stores and pet sections of large department stores: In the latter, you are most likely to find mongrel dwarf rabbits (see page 7). If you want to find a purebred dwarf rabbit, ask your pet dealer for addresses of local rabbit breeders.

Through a rabbit breeders' club (look for addresses in the American Rabbit Breeders Association's yearbook, which is a directory of all the members of the ARBA in the United States and elsewhere): This organization knows of sources of purebred young rabbits. Or visit a local rabbit show where you will be able to look

around for a pedigreed rabbit. Here breeders often sell off their excess stock for reasonable prices.

Important Questions to Ask When You Buy a Rabbit
How young a rabbit should you buy? Eight weeks is the ideal age. Baby rabbits start eating earlier, at four weeks, but their intestines don't fully adjust to solid food until the sixth week, and this is a critical stage for the animals. Conscientious breeders therefore leave the baby rabbits with their mother for another week or two. Selling tiny baby rabbits four weeks old in pet shops is considered a cruelty to animals, and you should not support the practice.

Is it healthy? A healthy rabbit always has a smooth, glossy coat. It is lively and active, unless it happens to be taking a rest. Depending on its temperament, it may hop shyly into a corner or come up curiously to sniff your hand. The ears will be in motion in either case, and it will show a lively interest in what is happening around it.

What should you watch out for? A sick rabbit usually sits apathetically in a corner, doesn't react to the sounds around it, and stares straight ahead with dull eyes.

Other signs:
- inflamed or tearing eyes;
- frequent sneezing or coughing;
- discharge from the nose;
- a distended belly that feels hard to the touch;
- disheveled, lusterless fur that may even show bare spots and is soiled on the abdomen and around the anus;
- brown discharge from the ears (canker), caused by mites.

Vacation Care

If it has sufficient water, dry food, and hay, a rabbit can easily be left alone in its cage for a day or two.

If you are going somewhere for several weeks, you can do one of the following:

Take the rabbit along: Car trips should be as short as possible; you should spend your vacation in an area with a moderate climate; and you should stay in one place that has an area where the rabbit can run free (rent a cottage, for instance).

Leave the rabbit at home: Ask someone you know and who has experience with rabbits to look after your pet. Make sure the animal has a chance to spend some time outside its cage; this is especially important if you have just one rabbit. Remind the caretaker to pet the rabbit every day.

Board the rabbit: Your pet dealer may be willing to board your rabbit, but make sure it will have a chance to move around outside of its cage at least once a day and that it will not be housed next to birds with loud voices.

Freshly groomed and ready for action.

Reminder: If you should travel abroad, get an official certificate of health for your rabbit from a veterinarian. Find out at the appropriate consulate what other papers may be required.

Not recommended and to be resorted to only if all else fails: Boarding your rabbit at an animal shelter or with a breeder where the rabbit will be left sitting alone in its cage all day, is not a good idea.

Everything a Rabbit Needs

A Shopping List of Things to Get:

- an indoor cage with a hay rack;
- a food dish and perhaps an automatic food dispenser;
- a water bottle for the cage and a water bowl for the indoor run or on the terrace;
- the grain mixture or pellets the rabbit is used to and a bag of hay;
- straw or other bedding to be spread in the cage;
- a plastic pan and cat litter to serve later as the rabbit's toilet; and
- a nest box—for the beginning, a cardboard box with an entry hole cut in one wall will do.

The Right Indoor Cage

A pet rabbit living indoors spends a lot of time in its cage. The cage therefore has to offer enough room for the rabbit to move around and should be no smaller than a certain size.

A plastic tray constitutes the cage bottom. If it measures 40 × 20 × 6 inches (100 × 50 × 15 cm), it can even accommodate two dwarf rabbits (see photo, page 12) or other rabbits of a small breed.

The upper part of the cage, which is made of wire, has to be removable and should, combined with the plastic bottom, be at least 18 inches (45 cm) high for the nest box to fit inside easily. Other features to look for are:

- The upper part should sit on the edge of the plastic tray, not on its floor, so that when you lift it up you won't pull out the straw along with it.
- A top that can be flipped open makes it easier to take the rabbit out of its cage. This is particularly useful with fidgety young animals.
- If there is a small door in one of the side walls, the rabbits can hop in and out of the cage on their own, as during their daily period of running free.

Not recommended are cages whose upper parts are made of plastic with only a small grate in the top for ventilation. This type of cage is harmful because the solid walls isolate the animals inside and keep them from hearing and smelling what is going on around them. In addition, such plastic cages can turn into regular hothouses if the sun shines on them or they are too close to a radiator. This causes the animals to suffer from overheating.

Food and Water Dishes

Hay rack: There are small wire hay racks that are open at the top and hook into the wire grating inside the cage, and there are bowl-shaped metal hay dispensers that hook onto the outside of the cage and are open only at the top and the side that faces the cage.

My tip: Use a wire hay rack but equip it with a wooden cover the rabbit can sit on. This way the rabbit will not get stuck in the rack if it jumps on top of the hay.

Food dish: A glazed earthenware bowl serves well. If the bowl narrows toward the top, this keeps the food from being kicked out. Plastic bowls are too light and get knocked over too easily. Rabbits also like to nibble on them, which is not good for their health.

A food hopper can be added and is used for grain. It hooks onto the cage wall and therefore does not get dirtied by urine or feces.

A nest box, which can do double duty as a birthing or kindling box, should measure about 14 × 14 × 12 inches (35 × 35 × 30 cm) and be equipped with an entry hole about 6 inches (15 cm) in diameter. Such a box is large enough for dwarf rabbits and small breeds.

A water bottle with a nipple is also hung from the grating of the cage and should be equipped with a double-ball valve to keep water from dripping into the cage. Water bowls should not be used inside indoor cages; the water gets dirtied too quickly and then becomes a breeding ground for bacteria.

Bedding

Bedding for small pets usually consists of a mixture of peat moss and wood shavings or of wood shavings only and is sold at most pet supply stores. It is soft and absorbent but tends to cling to the fur and is then carried around the apartment by the rabbit. For this reason it is not recom-

Five Golden Rules for Choosing the Right Spot for the Cage

What the rabbit needs	What is harmful	Where the cage should be
Quiet, protection, a sense of safety; a chance to retreat, for example, into the nest box	Permanent stress, noise from a loud radio (can cause fear), screaming children people running past the cage, TV in the same room (rabbits perceive sounds of ultrahigh frequencies, which are painful to them).	A quiet spot, as in a bedroom. If the rabbit is noisy at night, place the cage outside the bedroom door before you go to bed and cover it with a light cloth so that the animal will not be frightened and blinded if the light goes on suddenly.
Fresh air	Drafts, as when the cage stands directly on the floor or near an open window.	Somewhat raised, for example on a mattress; cover cage well when airing the room or let the rabbit run in another room while the windows are open
Moderate temperatures (for indoor rabbits)	Excessive heat; overheated, dry rooms.	Away from stoves and radiators; make sure the sun doesn't shine on the cage in the summer.
Daylight	Being housed in a dark room with only artificial light.	Light, but not directly in the sun.

mended for angora and other long-haired rabbits.

Straw makes an ideal bedding. You can get it at pet supply stores or from a farmer.

My tip: Use oat straw because it has not been run through a chopper and rabbits can therefore nibble on it without any danger of hurting themselves. The one drawback is that oat straw is not as absorbent as wheat straw and has to be changed somewhat more frequently. If you place a thick layer of newspapers underneath it, the papers will absorb the urine and also provide a nonslippery footing. However, if your rabbit starts nibbling, you have to do without the papers because printer's ink contains poisonous substances.

The Right Spot for the Cage
My rabbits spend the entire summer on the balcony. When it gets cold I move them into the apartment and place their cage where they feel comfortable and won't get sick. Their indoor cage is thus a haven of safety for them (see the table on page 11).

This indoor cage is large enough to accommodate two dwarf rabbits if necessary.

Important: Falling is bad for rabbits. So make sure that the cage is always locked and that it stands secure and well balanced, especially if you have it on a table.

The Rabbit Toilet

A rabbit should have a toilet for its daily run outside the cage or on the balcony. Plastic pans designed for cats but without a top work fine for rabbits. The side walls should be about 4 inches (10 cm) high. The size of the pan depends on the size of the rabbit: 12 × 6 inches (30 × 40 cm) is adequate for dwarf rabbits; 16 × 20 inches (40 × 50 cm), for small regular breeds.

For litter I recommend cat litter, which is absorbent and also suppresses odors. It is the most practical litter you can use, and rabbits enjoy digging in it. My dwarf rabbit Mohrle not only loves to dig in her litter box but also enjoys rolling in it.

A Nest and Kindling Box

A rabbit never feels as safe and protected as it does in a burrow it has dug. To provide such a refuge for your pet rabbit, you should set up a nest box for it, which will also serve as a birthing or kindling box for a pregnant doe. You can buy such boxes from rabbit breeders' supply firms or build one yourself out of 1/4-inch (5 mm) plywood or particle board (see drawing on page 10). For the first few weeks a solid, brown cardboard box with an entry hole cut into it will do.

Don't worry if your first efforts at construction don't turn out perfectly. I have built three nest boxes thus far, and even the last one is still not square. My rabbits don't seem to be bothered in the least. They like their boxes, raise their young in them, and seek refuge in them when "danger threatens." They even defend them if necessary.

A safe haven with a peephole.

My tip: If the roof of the box flips up, it is easier to clean the inside. When you put a preservative on the wood, make sure it is a safe one and doesn't contain formaldehyde (read the list of ingredients on the package).

If Your Rabbit Lives on the Terrace

If you have a terrace, let your rabbit enjoy it, too. You can either let it have its daily free run there or set things up so that it will be comfortable outside

In the photos:
A cage and nest box offer an indoor rabbit warmth and a sense of safety. The Thuringian dwarf rabbit (above) is three weeks old.

13

from the spring to the late fall. This requires some thinking ahead and some preparations:

The floor, which usually consists of cold concrete, should be covered with straw or rattan mats. These coverings of natural fiber look attractive, serve as insulation against the cold floor, and are inexpensive and easy to find (at craft shops and stores selling interior decorating supplies).

Safety: If your balcony does not have solid walls, your rabbit will sooner or later force its way between the balusters and fall to its death. You can make

This outdoor run (measuring 6 × 3 × 3 feet or 2 × 1 × 1 m) is large enough that up to three rabbits can move around in it. A run ideally should be placed under a tree that provides it with shade.

your balcony safe by stretching wire mesh along its outside walls, attaching it securely on the floor. The wire mesh should be at least 32 inches (80 cm) high. On my balcony, the balustrade starts several inches above the floor, and I have lined it all around with wooden boards. This way my rabbits

are protected from drafts and also have something to chew on.

Cats represent a real danger if the balcony is within their reach. That is why you should lock your rabbit in its cage if you are not there to keep an eye on it.

The sun: If the entire balcony is exposed to the sun, you have to set up a shady area to which the rabbit can retreat. Shade can be provided by a wooden cover or an awning. Without protection against the sun the rabbit may suffer heat stroke. The protective covering should also keep the rain out.

For the winter as well as for cool summer evenings you should build a warm hutch that offers protection against the cold, wetness, and snow. The run outside the hutch should also have a roof over it.

Don't forget to provide food and water dishes made of heavy earthenware and a pan with kitty litter.

A Run in the Garden

A rabbit, no matter how small, never feels as happy as when it can spend some time outside in a garden. Here it can hop around and nibble on tender greens. But watch out! If you take your eyes off your rabbit for even a moment it may disappear. Once it has made its way into the neighbor's garden you may have a hard time catching it again. However, if you have an outdoor run (see drawing) you can leave your rabbit in it unsupervised for an hour or two now and then. But such a run is not adequate for leaving the rabbit outdoors permanently or even for longer periods of time.

Everyday Life with a Rabbit

Acclimation of the Newcomer

Bring your new rabbit home by way of the most direct route. When you get home, place it in its cage, which should be equipped with the following:

- a thick layer of bedding on top of some newspapers;
- fresh but not too cold water in the water bottle;
- fragrant hay in the hay rack, and
- a welcoming array of items in the food dish, including some thick rolled oats, mixed grains, a piece of apple, and some parsley.

Don't forget to have a nest box ready to which the rabbit can retreat.

Now leave the newcomer alone for a couple of hours. After so many upsetting experiences—being torn from its familiar surroundings, separated from its siblings, transported, exposed to all kinds of strange sounds and smells—any animal needs time and quietude to regain its bearings. Just wait and you will see: Soon the rabbit will start sniffing with curiosity at everything new around it, and then it will eat and groom itself. These are signs that the animal is beginning to feel at ease in your home. If during the next few days you pick it up now and then, seat it in your lap, pet it, and talk to it quietly, the rabbit will gradually get used to your scent and your voice. Rabbits are animals that need physical contact; warmth and affection are essential to them, and it doesn't take long before they become tame.

Introduction to Other Pets

Anyone who has grown up, like me, with many different kinds of pets and deals with them professionally loves not just one kind of creature. So I kept wishing for a cat even though the attempt with Naughty had not worked out (see page 6). This time I was determined to do better, and together with breeders and experienced rabbit owners I developed a three-phase plan of how to get a rabbit to adjust to other pets (see page 18). This plan could also be called a personality or compatibility test because it gives you a chance to find out if the animals you wish to combine are capable of getting used to each other and of coexisting peacefully. If major difficulties arise early on, you had better not keep the new animal. A single pet, especially one that is used

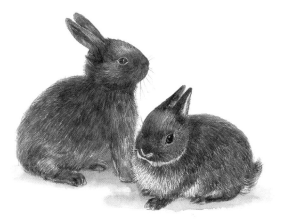

A purebred dwarf rabbit (right) is easy to tell from a mongrel (left). Purebred varieties have much shorter ears, a more massive head sitting directly on the cylindrical body, and short legs. These traits are easy to see even in young rabbits.

How fluffy and soft the fur of an Angora rabbit feels!

In the photos:
Rabbit friendships. To make sure there will be no mishaps, other pets—and small children as well—have to be given a chance to get acquainted gradually with the rabbit.

to being the center of attention, will find it hard to accept another animal and may react with excessive jealousy to any newcomer.

When chance brought us a little tomcat we named Robby, I hoped that things would work out this time if we proceeded according to my three-phase plan. Robby was a kitten that had been abandoned in the woods. Someone found it, sick and starving, and brought it to a friend of mine. The friend passed it on to me, saying: "Just for a little while until I find a new place

to live." As it turned out, Robby had found his new home—with us. He passed the adaptability test with flying colors and is the gentlest tomcat I have ever met. In the evening he loves to lie on the bed and watch our three little rabbits in their wild games and broken-field running. When one of them gets fresh and jumps up on the bed next to Robby, he sniffs it with interest and perhaps reaches out a paw. But he has never yet used his claws or tried to chase one of the rabbits and grab it by the nape. We almost wonder if Robby sensed somehow that this was one of the conditions for his staying with us.

Important: Don't start the three-phase plan until the rabbit feels at ease in your home and doesn't show any signs of shyness anymore. The first phase of the plan is the compatibility test which should be conducted before you commit yourself to keeping the second animal.

Rabbits and Children Become Friends

Rabbits are not Easter bunnies. But children associate Easter and colored eggs with the fuzzy little bunnies that fill cages by the hundreds in pet stores every year at this time. Well before *Watership Down*, Roger Rabbit, and Buggs Bunny, rabbits in picture books and films have charmed the hearts of children as well as adults. Because of the popularity of these fictional figures, people often buy rabbits in a rush of enthusiasm. But I am saddened every time I hear that rabbits have been taken to animal shelters or have simply been abandoned somewhere, and I have given some thought to why this happens. The reason why a child's love at first sight goes wrong so often is, I think, that animals and humans have different needs. We have to clarify, therefore, what the child is really wishing for, what the needs of the rabbit are, and how parents can help their children understand their pet better.

What children want is to have a bunny to pet and take along wherever they go, to play with it, and to have it at their disposal whenever they wish.

Rabbits need physical contact, closeness, and warmth, and they like to be petted. But they also need peace and quiet, and their freedom of move-ment should not be constantly inter-fered with. This means that only limited playing together is possible. From time to time parents will have to step in here on the animal's behalf.

Explain to the child that the rabbit should not be bothered while it eats, that it is not to be taken out of its cage when it would like to rest or sleep, and that it has to have one session a day when it is allowed to run free without interference. Also explain that rabbits don't chase balls and don't respond to a commanding whistle. Occasionally it may jump into your lap to be petted, and it will communicate in its own silent ways (see Rabbit Language—Body Language, page 50).

These two are getting along fine—but that is not always the case.

Three-phase Plan for Acquainting a Rabbit with Other Pets

A dog	A cat	A second rabbit

Phase 1: Getting used to the cage

A dog	A cat	A second rabbit
Lead the dog to the cage by the collar, talk to it calmly, pet it, praise it if it stays quiet and friendly; scold and say "No!" if it barks.	Let the cat loose in the room, pet it, talk to it lovingly, scold it if it tries to claw at the rabbit inside the cage, but don't shout or get excited. If the cat doesn't stop, squirt it briefly with water.	First place the two cages next to each other, later leave one rabbit in its cage and let the other one out. If the loose rabbit leaves scent marks and droppings around the cage, this is normal. Don't interfere.

Phase 2: Physical contact

A dog	A cat	A second rabbit
Put the rabbit on your lap so that it is at eye level with the dog. This is important or the dog will feel dominant. Let the dog sniff and lick, but if it is aggressive, scold it sharply and yank it back by the collar. Otherwise praise and pet both animals.	Take the rabbit on your lap and place the cat next to it. Pet both animals and let each sniff the smell of the other on your hand so they can study the new smell and get used to it.	Put both rabbits on your lap, pet them, let them sniff each other, and get a gentle hold of the dominant one with your hand, so that it will not bite the other.

Phase 3: Running loose together as soon as the animals have demonstrated their compatability

A dog	A cat	A second rabbit
Let the rabbit run free in the room, and take the dog up to it on the leash. Talk to the dog soothingly, pet it, and let go of it if it is calm and friendly. Don't let the dog chase the rabbit; this would scare the rabbit half to death.	Let the cat approach the rabbit on a leash. This is a difficult exercise because a hopping rabbit triggers a cat's play and hunting instinct. Don't let the cat loose until it no longers tries to pursue the rabbit.	Let both of them run free with lots of room to get away from each other. If serious biting ensues, remove the dominant animal. My rabbits have all learned to get along after fighting to establish their places in the rank order.

No matter how solid the friendship may seem between your rabbit and another pet—such as a dog or cat—you should still be close by whenever the rabbit is outside its cage.

Children often think that their pets will like what they themselves like. But that is not so. Rabbits should not be given candy or even the most delicious chocolate bar. A rabbit would also be happier if the newest rock hits were played at a somewhat lower volume. And it won't appreciate at all being tucked under an arm like a teddy bear (see Picking Up and Carrying a Rabbit Correctly, page 22).

Be consistent and teach your child to share responsibility for feeding and taking care of the animal, cleaning its quarters, and doing whatever other small chores are required. This is the only way a child can learn an important lesson for later life, namely, that to love someone means being there for that someone, even at times when you don't feel like it.

How Will My Rabbit Get Housebroken?

Rabbits are by nature clean animals. Wild rabbits urinate and defecate only in certain places, and pet rabbits, too, always use the same corner of their cage for this purpose. What is tricky is to get your rabbit to use a certain spot—the litter box—when it runs free indoors or on the terrace.

This is how you go about it:
- Set up a plastic pan with kitty litter in the room the very first time the rabbit is allowed to run free. Put a few of its droppings in the litter.
- Place the rabbit in the pan, and don't give up if it hops out the first time and uses the carpet instead.
- Place the litter box in a favorite corner, perhaps underneath a corner bench or in some other out-of-the-way spot.
- Keep placing the animal in the litter box, and where accidents have happened wipe spots well with diluted vinegar. The vinegar acts as a disinfectant and its smell is abhorrent to the sensitive nose of a rabbit.

Other measures you can take:

Tip number 1: Let the rabbit out of its cage several times a day for about 20 minutes rather than for one longer period of an hour or so. Rabbits are not long-distance runners and prefer to spread their activity over several shorter sessions. This way they won't leave droppings all over the place but usually defecate after they return to their cage.

Tip number 2: If possible, schedule the exercise period before meals. Then the urge to relieve itself won't be so great. I let my rabbits run free in our large kitchen in the morning, the afternoon, and the evening and reward them with a small treat when I return them to the cage. This makes being caught seem less like "punishment."

Important: Never shout at your rabbit or smack it, no matter how lightly.

Rabbits rise up on their haunches when they want to get a better view of their surroundings and sometimes to indicate that they would like to be let in or out of their cage.

Set up a home for your rabbit on the balcony; a wire-mesh partition allows the animal to be part of family life but keeps it from hopping around your home constantly.

First there is active scratching in the litter.

Using the litter box is contagious.

You would only upset or scare the animal, without furthering your house-breaking efforts in the least. By the way, rabbit droppings don't smell; they are dry and can easily be vacuumed up.

Eating feces: The feces you sometimes see rabbits ingest are excretions from the cecum that contain significant amounts of vitamin B1 and protein. These special excretions are important for the animals' health and are usually picked up and swallowed directly from the anus. They are kidney-shaped, moist and shiny, have a slightly sweetish smell, and are sometimes stuck together like a miniature bunch of grapes. Normal rabbit droppings are dry and round.

The Daily Free Run

Rabbits like to hop about, dash around like broken-field runners, leap into the air, and disappear like a shot in some hiding place. They also love jumping up on something soft, such as a pile of sofa cushions, and snuggling down there in blissful comfort. All these things you can, of course, watch only if you let your pet rabbit run free as much as possible every day, at least 20 minutes three times a day or once or twice for a longer period. An animal that is cooped up all day in a cage needs a chance to make full use of its body without physical restrictions. This helps it develop its sensory capacities, allows for the full expression of its personality, and benefits the heart, lungs, and muscles. Rabbits that have plenty of opportunity to run free stay healthier and live longer.

Preparations:
• Do not keep valuable carpets and furniture in the room where the rabbit runs free, or they may be gnawed at or dirtied.
• Do not leave any electric wires exposed. Rabbits sometimes nibble on them, which can prove fatal. Telephone wires are also favorite items for chewing on.
• Make sure there is always a litter box in the room.
• Offer a varied environment. Have some chairs and sofas for jumping up on and leaping down from, some nooks and crannies underneath bureaus and book shelves for hiding in, and set up empty cartons with cutout doors for crawling into.

A rabbit in the act of "doing its business."

Sources of danger:
- Smooth parquet or linoleum floors or cold tile floors: rabbits can slip on them or catch cold.
- Doors: open and shut them slowly to make sure no rabbit is squashed by accident.
- Human feet: rabbits sometimes jump between one's feet.

If you let your rabbit run on the balcony or in the garden, you should watch out for the dangers I mentioned on page 14.

My tip: Don't let a rabbit explore your entire home on its first venture outside the cage. Rabbits are territorial, and one room is enough turf for the beginning. Only when the rabbit feels fully at home in this room and moves around in it in complete comfort should other rooms, the balcony, or the garden be opened up for exploration. Too much new territory all at once is overwhelming, causing insecurity and anxiety.

Outings
If you are not lucky enough to have a garden but would like to do something special for your rabbit, I suggest an excursion into nature. Pick a point of destination according to the following considerations:
- Avoid parks where dogs roam freely. Rabbits can pick up diseases if they eat plants where dogs have urinated. There is also the danger that a dog that is not on a leash may chase and hurt your rabbit or cause is to run away.

Place the rabbit on your arm in such a way that your other hand remains on the animal's nape. Then you can grab hold quickly if the rabbit should try to leap down.

In the photos:
Training for housebreaking. Get your rabbit accustomed to using the right spot, its litter box, from the very first day. These two dwarf rabbits are already trained at six weeks.

21

• Fields in the countryside are a better bet, especially if they are easy to survey. In the summer there should be a nearby tree to offer shade. I always take along something to read or a snack and allow plenty of time.

When picking up a rabbit, get a secure hold of the skin between the shoulder blades and immediately support the rear end with your left hand.

A brush for grooming. Especially during molting season, you should brush your rabbit vigorously every other day.

It is impossible to train a rabbit to go for a walk like a dog. A rabbit refuses to hop along behind you obediently. Handling a rabbit on a leash requires a great deal of sensitivity and experience.

Picking Up and Carrying a Rabbit Correctly

There is hardly anything that is done incorrectly as often by rabbit owners as picking up and carrying the animal.

The right way: Get a secure hold of the rabbit with your right hand just behind the shoulder blades and lift it up while supporting it with your left hand. Always place and hold the rabbit on your arm in such a way that one hand stays on the animal's nape. This allows you to grab a hold of it at any moment if you need to. Children, too, can be taught how to do this.

The wrong way: Tucking a rabbit under your arm like a teddy bear. This is not only uncomfortable for the animal but also harmful because ribs can get broken and internal organs injured. If the animal starts to wriggle, it may fall to the ground and get hurt. Unfortunately, such accidents are not uncommon.

Note: Pulling a rabbit by its ears is considered cruelty to animals.

Necessary Grooming

Rabbits usually keep themselves very clean, and there is no need to give them baths. Sometimes a sweetish smelling secretion collects around the sexual opening. This can be wiped off gently with a soft cloth and a little oil or lukewarm water. There are just a few other grooming chores that should be performed.

The coat: During molting, the rabbit should be brushed vigorously every other day with a brush with bristles that are not too hard. This helps remove the dead hair. Brushing is also recommended once a week to stimulate circulation. Angora rabbits have to be shorn every three months; this is absolutely essential for their comfort and health.

The teeth: A rabbit's teeth never stop growing and have to get enough wear in order not to get too long. The best thing is to make sure that the rabbit always has lots of hay, dry bread, and branches for gnawing. Teeth that are too long interfere with eating. If a rabbit has an abnormal occlusion, the teeth have to be shortened regularly by the veterinarian (see drawing, page 59).

The toenails: In most cases the toenails don't get enough wear because a rabbit that is kept indoors doesn't have enough opportunity to dig. The nails then grow too long, curl inward, and interfere with locomotion. That is why they should be checked every two or three months and trimmed by the veterinarian or a pet dealer. You can also learn how to do this yourself (see drawing).

• When you trim the nails, always use special nail clippers that prevent splintering of the nails (available at pet supply stores).

• Place the rabbit in your lap, take hold of one foot and push the fur back a little. The front feet have five toes, one of them on the side of the leg; the back feet have four.

• Cut off only the tips, a good 1/4 of an inch (1/2 cm) below the live part of the nail. In light-colored nails it is easy to see the blood vessels and nerves.

• Be careful not to cut in the wrong place. An incorrect cut hurts the animal and causes bleeding.

• If your rabbit has dark toenails, ask someone to help you. The other person can shine a flashlight at the nail from below so that you can see better which part is alive. The second person is also useful in handling a struggling rabbit, helping you hold it, petting and soothing it. I always ask one of my children to help me, and they have become quite good at it by now.

Cleaning the Cage and the Accessories

Bedding: Fluff it up a little every day with your hand, and change it every three to four days. Don't wait longer or it will begin to smell. Because I always put some newspapers underneath the bedding, I simply roll up the dirty bedding in the papers like a sausage and put it in the trash like that.

My tip: Gardeners should be sure to compost the rabbit dung and the straw.

The dung contains high amounts of nitrogen, potash, phosphorus, and lime; it doesn't harm earthworms and breaks down quickly.

The plastic bottom pan: Clean it thoroughly with warm water and a mild household cleanser, then dry well. There is no need to disinfect it except in cases of sickness.

Food dishes and water: Try to rinse them clean every other day with water. Scrub the water bottle with a bottle brush to keep algae from forming in it.

Hold the nail clippers with the spring-loaded handle pointing downward and make your cut at a safe distance from the blood vessels.

An indoor rabbit doesn't have much chance to dig, so that its claws are not worn down enough and have to be trimmed regularly. But don't cut them too short because that causes the animal pain.

Note: For hygienic reasons you should always use a separate brush and cloth to clean the rabbit's things.

Diet

What Rabbits Like to Eat

Rabbits should get a grain mixture, greens and succulent foods, and hay once every day. On such a diet they will stay healthy and vigorous for a long time. The other thing to keep in mind is that rabbits are little gourmets who like variety in their menu, with each animal developing its own special likes and dislikes. My dwarf rabbit Mümmi, for instance, likes a strawberry now and then, whereas Mohrle has a special weakness for parsley; and Dicki, the Angora, will ignore everything else if there are some tender fennel stalks.

Wild rabbits and hares, too, have food preferences, and these don't always meet with the approval of farmers and gardeners. The department of parks and public gardens of Munich, for instance, issued a directive to stop planting crocus and cineraria in the Hofgarten park because every spring the wild rabbits in that area cleaned up every single plant as it came up. And an organic farmer from Ohio told me that his field of soybeans had hordes of rabbits in it. Apparently word had gotten around among the rabbits that young soybean plants, especially when they haven't been sprayed, are a special delicacy.

Commercial Rabbit Feeds

Commerical rabbit feeds (the so-called pellets) that satisfy all the animals' nutritional needs are sold at pet shops and the pet sections of large department stores. They contain everything a rabbit needs, such as different kinds of grains, as well as hay, seeds and vitamins, minerals, and amino acids. Pellets also contain coccidiostats, which is a drug that reduces the odds of rabbits contracting coccidiosis. (This disease is caused by coccidia, microscopic protozoa that live in the epithelium of the intestines and destroy it.) These pellets are essential to a healthy diet and should never be lacking in commercial feeds. My rabbits seem to be quite oblivious of this fact. They always leave the pellets in the dish and seem to prefer hay in its natural form. They are, after all, gourmets and not fast-food freaks.

Unfortunately, these commercial rabbit feeds don't contain enough cracked and rolled grains, and I therefore always add some thick whole-grain flakes (oats and different kinds of wheat). Rabbits like these flakes and also digest them better and more efficiently than unbroken grains. But I am not suggesting that you experiment by making up your own grain mixtures. To do that you need detailed knowledge about the nutritional needs of rabbits, and nutritional deficiencies lead to health problems.

Greens and Succulent Foods

The most natural and the healthiest kind of food for rabbits has always been and still is greens and succulent foods. Wild greens, vegetables, and fruit are rich in proteins and calcium and are very nutritious. Don't let believers in commercial feeds convince you otherwise. Anyone who says greens and succulent foods cause rabbits to become obese and sick is not feeding the animals properly (see Ten Golden Rules of Correct Feeding, page 28).

A wire hay rack that is hung from the bars of the cage.

A water bottle allows the rabbit to drink whenever it wants to.

Carrots are the favorite food of rabbits—even this four-week old.

Wild plants that are good for rabbits: dandelion greens, common and English plantain, yarrow, comfrey, pigweed, orache, alfalfa, yellow clover, and young nettle shoots. Collect only plants you know!

Be careful with red clover because it causes bloating. Mix only small amounts into the food and don't harvest before it is in bloom.

Poisonous plants are: fool's parsley, hemlock, belladonna, common nightshade, laburnum, and yew. Don't count on a rabbit's instinct to determine what is good or bad for it. Never feed any of these plants.

Suitable items from the kitchen and garden: Carrots, carrot tops, corn salad, chicory, endive, radish greens, celery, celeriac, kohlrabi with the leaves, fennel, Swiss chard, leaves from pea plants, sunflowers, Jerusalem artichokes, apples, pears, and, when they are in season, a strawberry or a raspberry now and then.

Herbs like parsley, mustard greens,

25

Suggested Feeding Plan, Including Amounts and Feeding Times

Time	Young rabbits	Dwarf rabbits	Mongrels and small breeds
	up to three months	up to 3 pounds (1.5 kg)	up to 6.5 pounds (3 kg)
Morning	Commerical food: .5 to .7 ounce (15–20 g)	Commercial food: .7 to 1 ounce (20–30 g)	Commercial food: 1 to 1.8 ounces (30–50 g)
Every second or third day add:	Thick wholewheat grain wheat or oat flakes: 1 teaspoon	Thick wholewheat grain wheat or oat flakes: 1 tablespoon	Thick wholewheat grain wheat or oat flakes: 2–3 tablespoons
Afternoon or early evening	.9 ounce (25 g) greens, e.g., corn salad, fennel, parsley, chicory; in the summer dandelion greens or alfalfa	.7 to 1.3 ounces (20–35 g) greens or up to 2 ounces (60 g) green vegetables and carrots, kohlrabi, celerirac or fennel	up to 3 ounces (90 g) greens (2 handfuls) or up to 6 ounces (180 g) green vegetables and carrots, kohlrabi, celeriac, fennel, and so on
Daily	Supply as much hay as the rabbit will eat in 24 hours		
Once a week (things to nibble)	Dry bread: .9 ounce (25 g)	Dry bread: 1 to 1.3 ounces (30–35 g)	Dry bread: up to 1.8 ounces (50 g or about 1½ slices)
	If the rabbit is getting too fat, substitute hardtack for the dry bread. Give your rabbit as many twigs as it wants and, in the fall, dry leaves.		
Once a week	Fruit: ¼ of an apple or pear	Fruit: ¼ of an apple or pear	Fruit: ½ of an apple or pear

Rabbits are individualists as far as food is concerned. What one enjoys, another may reject. You will soon know which things your rabbit likes best. But don't offer just certain foods. Rabbits stay healthy only if they get a varied diet.

sage, caraway, borage, savory, dill, and lovage are especially good for rabbits.

Not so good are raw potatoes, lettuce (especially lettuce that is grown in hothouses and may have high nitrate residues), as well as all kinds of cabbage because they tend to cause bloating. It is alright to give your rabbit small amounts of Chinese cabbage, brussels sprouts, and cauliflower now and then.

Avoid raw beans and sprouted potatoes; the beans and potato sprouts are poisonous.

Hay, the Basic Staple

Hay is essential for a rabbit's digestion. Always put enough into the hay rack to last until the next day. You can buy hay packed in small bags at pet shops. Or you can get large bags or bales from a farmer.

Watch out for the following when buying hay:

High-quality hay consists of young grasses, clover, and other plants. It has an aromatic smell and is greenish.

Hay from a second cutting is finer and thus suitable for a convalescent diet.

Poor-quality hay is either too old or lacks plants other than grass, especially the valuable herbs. Old hay is very dusty, which irritates the sensitive air passages of a rabbit and makes it sneeze. Old hay has also lost much of its nutritive value. You should not buy yellowish hay, either, because it consists of dried up, woody grasses that rabbits can't digest well.

Caution: Hay should not be fed to rabbits fresh from the field because it causes colic.

Things to Nibble and Gnaw On

Rabbits have to be able to gnaw enough to keep their constantly growing teeth worn down properly. You can give them dried bread crusts to chew on now and then if the bread is not moldy, too salty, or spicy. If you are worried about calories you can substitute hardtack. Pet stores also have various nibbling treats for rabbits. Another good idea is to bring home some twigs from a walk in the woods, especially ones with buds and young shoots from hazelnut bushes, fruit trees, willows, and spruce or fir trees.

Caution: Don't offer any sprayed twigs for nibbling or ones that are still frozen.

Medicinal Herbs or Weeds

Rabbits suffering from minor ailments or from serious illnesses respond especially well to medicinal herbs.

Nettles are considered a noxious weed by many gardeners, but they

A rabbit lying in this position would like to rest and be left undisturbed.

contain significant amounts of calcium, iron, phosphorus, and protein. They are also high in vitamin D and help strengthen bones, cleanse the blood, and stimulate the metabolism. Feed the entire plant fresh, but let it wilt a little first so that it won't sting as much. Nettle hay is a good food for winter.

Yarrow is familiar to many in the form of an herb tea that settles the stomach, counteracts inflammation,

Nibbling on some commercial food.

Taking a few bites of juicy pear.

and relieves cramps. For rabbits, yarrow is especially effective against bloating and intestinal problems. You should always have some yarrow, either fresh or dried, to add to a rabbit's food and for medicinal purposes.

The Importance of Drinking Water

Unfortunately one hears again and again that "rabbits don't need water." That is not the case at all. Rabbits don't sweat like humans and have to regulate their body temperature through increased breathing and greater intake of fluids. It is also incorrect to assume that succulent foods are a substitute for water. Leave it up to your rabbit when and how much it wants to drink. It should always have access in the cage to a water bottle that is filled every day with fresh water. The water should not be ice cold; room temperature, 65–68° F (18–20° C), is best.

Note: Rabbits drink more than usual on hot days, in dry, heated rooms, or if they eat almost exclusively dry commercial food. Nursing does and Angora rabbits also need more water.

Ten Golden Rules for Correct Feeding

1. Always give greens and succulent foods fresh. Anything left over after ten minutes should be removed from the cage; otherwise it might wilt, ferment, rot, or get moldy. Spoiled greens can give rise to serious illness. Always put hay in the rack to keep it from getting dirty and contaminated.

2. Don't make any abrupt changes in a rabbit's diet. If you use mostly dry rabbit food, don't switch suddenly to fresh things in the spring.

3. Wash vegetables and fruit well, shake well, and let remaining water drip off.

4. Don't give any food directly from the refrigerator.

5. Never give a rabbit frozen, canned, or cooked vegetables.

6. Don't collect greens for your rabbit by the side of the road (danger of lead poisoning) or in parks where dogs relieve themselves (possible transmission of pathogens).

7. Provide plenty of variety in the diet. Give small amounts at a time and add some greens; and make sure there is plenty of hay. This way you won't have to worry about digestive problems.

Vegetables are the best.

8. Feed your rabbit at regular times. A rabbit's stomach very quickly gets used to a feeding routine.

9. Make sure your rabbit gets plenty of exercise, so that it will stay lively and healthy. If it is getting too fat, introduce one fasting day a week. This won't harm the animal. Give only water and hay on this day. Obese rabbits are subject to heart disease and die young.

10. It is best to gather greens on meadows and fields that are not under active cultivation and have conse-quently not been treated with fertilizers, pesticides, and herbicides. Also refrain from using chemicals in your own garden—for your own sake as well as your rabbit's.

In the photos:
Lots of different kinds of food. Rabbits that are kept properly eat only as much as their bodies need; they don't overeat out of boredom the way animals that live in constant confinement do.

If Your Rabbit Gets Sick

Keeping Rabbits Healthy

Rabbits are by nature robust, undemanding, and resistant animals. If it is housed properly and taken good care of, a healthy rabbit without hereditary weaknesses rarely gets sick. By observing the feeding rules given in the previous chapter, making sure the animal gets plenty of exercise, setting up the cage in a good location and

Injuries sustained if a rabbit is stepped on or caught in a door can sometimes result in paralysis.

keeping it clean and dry, and treating the animal with affection and understanding, you will have done much to keep your rabbit healthy. But because a rabbit can't tell us when it is sick, it is up to you, the animal's keeper, to detect the first signs of possible illness in time and to initiate the proper measures (see checklist, page 58). But don't attempt to act as the animal's veterinarian.

What You Can Do Immediately

If your rabbit is not feeling well and is suffering from some minor ailment, you should do something about it as quickly as possible. Often all that is needed is to correct the situation that is giving rise to the problem, and the rabbit will resume its usual lively ways. By acting on the following suggestions you may save yourself a trip to the veterinarian.

Treatment for light diarrhea: Change the bedding frequently and keep the animal warm. If you also give the rabbit lukewarm camomile tea and some boiled, unsalted rice, the diarrhea should subside within at most two days. If it doesn't, take the animal to the veterinarian.

Treatment for minor constipation: Stop feeding grain and provide plenty of liquids. Try giving the rabbit caraway tea or a teaspoonful of olive oil. Also make sure that the animal is getting exercise. If there is no relief within 24 hours, take the rabbit to the veterinarian.

Treatment of allergic sniffling: Eliminate the cause, such as dusty hay or caustic cleansers that emit harmful fumes. In case of doubt, take the animal to the veterinarian.

Emergency treatment for heat stroke: Move the rabbit to the shade immediately and offer it water at room temperature. Cool it down by applying damp but not ice cold compresses first to the head, then to the legs. Feed it some coffee to stimulate circulation ($^{1}/_{2}$ teaspoon for a baby rabbit, 1 teaspoon for dwarf rabbits, 1 to 2 teaspoons for small breeds).

Rabbits as Patients

There is hardly a more long-suffering and quiet patient than a rabbit. Even when in acute pain, it doesn't whine or complain. You can tell the suffering only from the look in its eyes; and the course of a disease is apparent only in some changes of behavior and appearance. Take note of the following points when nursing a sick rabbit and also to help your veterinarian diagnose and treat a disease:

• When did you first notice any changes of behavior in the animal?
• Has it been eating? If yes, when, what, and how much?
• What does its stool look like? Is the animal constipated or does it have diarrhea?
• Feed the sick rabbit a convalescent diet. For some disorders, fasting is best.
• Be especially careful that there is no noise or activity near the cage.
• Changes in temperature, drafts, and other forms of stress are particularly harmful now and tend to aggravate the condition. Avoid them at all cost.
• Observe the strictest hygiene. In case of infectious diseases, change the bedding frequently and disinfect the cage and accessories (use One-Stroke Envioron: a half-ounce per gallon [15 ml per 3.8 l] of water, or another biological disinfectant).
• As a precaution you should isolate the sick animal and put it in a cage by itself, away from other rabbits and preferably in a different room.
• Don't react with anger if the rabbit, in a state of confusion, should bite you out of pain or fright. Treat the animal with understanding; it needs you more than ever now.

Putting a Rabbit to Sleep

It is a sad fact that, in spite of veterinary care and our best nursing efforts, pets sometimes die or have to be put to sleep. Such a death is painful and makes us humans realize that we have lost not just an animal but a friend, a member of the family who has grown close to our hearts over the years. But sickness is not always the cause of death; sometimes faulty breeding is the responsible factor. My yellow Angora rabbit Dicki was only one and one half years old when he suddenly fell over while hopping around in apparently perfect health. The veterinarian discovered from some X rays he took that the animal was suffering from congenital degenerative changes of the spinal cord. The resulting obstruction of the nerve passages led first to impaired locomotion and evenually to complete paralysis. The situation deteriorated in spite of vitamin treatments, and one day, when I could no longer bear the look in the animal's eyes as it sadly watched the others hop around, I took it to the veterinarian to have it put to sleep. Mohrle, the dwarf rabbit, clearly mourned for Dicki and hardly ate anything for about a week.

Rabbits kept properly rarely get sick. At times when their normal resistance is lowered, as during molting season and pregnancy, they need especially good care.

Rabbits stretch like cats after they have been resting. This is a habit found in all lagomorphs but not in rodents.

Breeding and Propagation

If Your Pet Rabbit Is to Have Babies

- Do you and your family have enough time to take proper care of the pregnant doe and later the offspring?
- Do you have plans to go on vacation or to move, or is some exceptionally busy time ahead of you in the next couple of months? If so, you had better postpone the happy event. Gestation takes about one month, and the babies need care for about two months.
- Is the indoor cage large enough to accommodate the kindling box as well as the mother rabbit and her active offspring?
- If you are planning to keep one or more of the baby rabbits, can you prepare additional quarters in good time (a separate cage, a second hutch)?
- If you plan on finding homes for the young rabbits, will you start exploring the possibilities early (relatives, pet shops, organizations for the humane treatment of animals)? It is not always easy to find places where the animals will be in good hands.
- Before you breed your rabbit have you discussed with your children that you are *not* planning to keep the baby rabbits (otherwise there are bound to be tears)?
- If you plan to raise more than one litter, do you have specialized knowl-

edge, lots of time, and adequate space? An apartment with a balcony is not big enough for this hobby. If you hope to raise a certain breed of rabbit, you should join a rabbit breeders' club. There you will find experienced breeders who can advise you, offer practical help, and assist in finding rabbits of the desired breed. Breeding rabbits that match the breed standard requires a lot of experience and detailed knowledge about the genetics of selective breeding and about the breed.

Selecting the Parent Animals

Regardless of what kind of rabbits you want to breed, you have to observe two rules: The future parents have to be healthy, and they should be of proper breeding age. Rabbits mature sexually at the early age of twelve weeks, and male siblings have to be separated from female ones at that time, but they

Thuringian dwarf lop. The striking features of this breed are its long, drooping ears, measuring from 9¹/₂ to 11 inches (24–28 cm), and its lively temperament.

Two rabbits that haven't met before start out by sniffing each other thoroughly to find out if they want to be friends.

should not be bred until later. If does are mated too early they can suffer permanent damage.

The right age: Small breeds should be at least six months old before breeding; medium-size breeds, seven months; and large breeds, at least eight months old. These are general guidelines; the developmental stage of the individual animals should also be taken into account.

Note: Don't experiment by mating animals that are too dissimilar. The

Rabbits that like each other huddle together and lick each other's heads.

male should preferably be somewhat smaller than the female. If you are raising dwarf rabbits, you should make sure that the parents exhibit the desired breed characteristics, but you don't need to worry about combining colors. Sometimes you get colorful surprises that are charming.

If you are trying to meet the breed standard you have to use purebred animals of the same breed, that is, rabbits you have obtained from a breeder and that are entered in their breed's register and have an identifying tattoo.

Sexual Receptivity

In many species, the animals are sexually excited and ready to mate only at certain times. In the case of cats and dogs, for instance, we speak of estrus or heat. In these animals, the female's sexual receptivity is periodic and lasts only a short time. Female rabbits, by contrast, are sexually receptive almost the entire year. Sometimes the mere presence of a buck nearby is enough to bring a doe into heat, and it may even give rise to false pregnancy. In this state, a doe will gather straw, carry it in her mouth to the kindling box, keep digging frantically in the bedding, and sometimes act aggressively toward other females in the group. But don't let yourself be fooled by this behavior! The only reliable signs of a true pregnancy are a very round belly, teats that are visibly enlarged, and, shortly before the babies are due, the doe pulling hair from her abdomen to line the nest (see The Approaching Birth, page 36).

The Mating

I give my rabbits the opportunity to mate while they are running free outside the cage. This gives me a chance to observe their natural behavior: the buck's stiff-legged walk as he circles the doe, the mutual affectionate licking, the playful chasing after each other. If you want the mating to take place inside the cage you always have to put the doe in with the buck, never the other way around. If you placed the buck in the doe's cage, he would feel very insecure; and the doe, if she is aggressive, may bite him. Once the doe is ready to mate, she lies down and "presents" herself by raising her rear end.

Copulation usually happens very quickly and lasts at most 15 seconds. After ejaculating, the male slides off the doe to the side, often with a short growling sound, and lies there exhausted for a few seconds. It is pointless to try to force a mating, as by tying the doe's tail up. Just treat the animals with patience and love, let them take their time, and don't get upset if it turns out that your doe wants nothing to do with a certain buck. Between rabbits, too, there is not always sympathy but also occasional antipathy.

The Pregnant Doe

It takes 28 to 31 days from the day of conception to the birth, or kindling. If a litter is exceptionally large, a doe may give birth earlier. If a litter consists only of one or two rabbits, they are usually quite large, and the kindling may be delayed until 35 days after the mating. Unfortunately, overdue baby rabbits are often stillborn.

Signs: In the course of pregnancy, the doe begins to dig restlessly in her bedding. She burrows everywhere, trying to build a nest. She may also behave differently, becoming nervous and shy, for instance, and perhaps even scratching. Especially during the last few days she may lie there with her head raised high, panting.

Death of the fetuses: Fetuses dying in the womb is a phenomenon that occurs among rabbits and that has not yet been scientifically explained. It is a form of birth control that has been observed in wild as well as domestic rabbits. All that we know so far is that the death is not due to some disease or hormonal malfunctioning. Scientists suspect that it is a reaction on the part of these highly sensitive animals to excessive environmental stress. It is one more reason for treating a pregnant doe with special care and consideration.

Four Golden Rules for Treating a Pregnant Doe

1. Diet: You should feed your doe especially nutritious and varied food during this time. Add calcium and vitamin supplements (available at pet stores) to her diet, and make sure she has access to fresh water 24 hours a day.

2. Handling: Pick the animal up only if absolutely necessary. This applies especially to the last couple of weeks. Never let the doe dangle when you pick her up by the nape of her neck but always support her rear end immediately with your other hand. A tame doe remains friendly during pregnancy and will let you pet her. But sometimes she may appear nervous, and she may respond timidly or aggressively to

A pregnant doe collects hay and straw to build a nest for her young. Sometimes does in heat also start building a nest.

strange people or animals. This is normal and only a passing phase.

3. Behavior toward other rabbits: If you have several female rabbits you should keep the pregnant doe away from the others because she will almost inevitably become aggressive toward them. This is not a sign of meanness; the animal is simply protecting its nesting place (burrow, cage) against rivals. My female rabbit Mohrle even bit a six-week-old little rabbit's nose once, something she would never do under ordinary circumstances. A pregnant

Three-day-old white-tipped black dwarf rabbits.

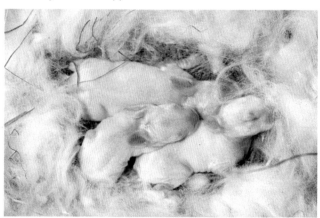

Three-day-old white Angoras.

female's behavior toward males, on the other hand, can be very varied. She may get into fights with an importunate buck (a reaction triggered by a hormone produced by the corpus luteum) but be perfectly content in the presence of a castrated male or one that does not behave aggressively. She will even cuddle up to him and let him lick her.

4. The quarters: Don't move the cage when the doe gets pregnant but leave it in its usual place. Keep noise and stress down to a minimum; try to keep screaming children away; and don't slam doors.

The Approaching Birth

About ten days before the due date you should put an extra large amount of bedding and hay in the cage. If the cage doesn't yet contain a nest box, you now have to provide a box to serve as a kindling box. Almost any doe will go to work immediately inside the box. Having a box satisfies the ancient need of rabbits to deliver their young hidden away in a dark place. The box also serves to protect the young from the cold and drafts and keeps them from crawling out into the open too early.

A few days before the birth, the doe begins to pluck fur from her belly to line her nest. She lies down to rest more often, and her swollen belly indicates that the time for delivery is approaching. Perhaps you have noted the mating date on your calendar so that you have a fairly exact idea of when the kindling should take place.

The Young Arrive

Rabbits deliver their young without any outside help, unlike cats and dogs, which often wait to have a trusted human nearby before they give birth. These more dependent pets appreciate encouraging support and petting during the birth process, as well as obstetric assistance if necessary. Rabbits on the other hand are so efficient and quiet that I haven't to this day succeeded at witnessing the exciting event.

The last time one of my does was about to give birth I was determined to be present, so I sat in front of the cage very quietly for four hours. The doe was staying inside her box and had stopped eating. But just as I noticed that the labor pains were setting in, the telephone rang. I made the mistake of answering and getting involved in a

My dwarf doe Mohrle with her three-and-a-half-week-old offspring.

conversation that lasted a quarter of an hour. When I came back to the cage, it was too late. The doe had delivered one young after the other, licked the naked little creatures, severed the umbilical cord, and eaten the afterbirth so that the nest was nice and clean. By now the baby rabbits were already nursing, as I could tell from their contented sucking noises.

It happens occasionally that a doe will partially eat one of her young. I saw this once with a very timid and nervous doe that I was temporarily taking care of. After a difficult, overdue birth, during which she must have pulled the baby bunny out by the leg, she got carried away licking the amniotic membrane off and chewing through the umbilical cord. She kept on chewing, with the result that one ear and one leg were crippled. Theories have been suggested, but the causes of this maternal "cannibalism" still await explanation.

In the photos:
The early development of young rabbits. Thanks to the nutritiousness of the doe's milk, which is very high in protein and fat, baby rabbits double their birth weight in only seven days. 37

The visible swelling of the doe's teats is an infallible sign of pregnancy.

The Nest Check

After the kindling you should check the nest cautiously. Pet the doe to calm her and, if necessary, lure her out of the cage by offering her a treat. Now take the top off the nest box, gently move the hay and wool aside, and check to see if all the young are healthy and without injuries. If there are remains of afterbirth or stillborn young, they have to be removed. If a doe is young or very nervous, she may have neglected to move one or more young into the warm nest, and you will have to do it for her right away. Naked little baby rabbits are extremely dependent on warmth and die of cold very quickly if they are left outside the nest. Check the nest again after two or three days. Healthy and well-fed baby rabbits have full, round little bellies. If the bellies are sunken and the skin over them is loose and floppy, the babies will die within a couple of days because they are either sick or too weak. Newly born rabbits decline very rapidly because does nurse their young only twice a day. You can attempt to give them extra feedings, but this is not very easy (see Bottle Feeding Baby Rabbits, page 39)
.

The Development of Baby Rabbits

First week: Rabbits are nidicoulous (that is, they need the protection of a nest during the first days of their life) and are born blind, deaf, and completely naked. Lying together in the warm nest they help keep each other warm and are nursed by the mother doe twice a day. The colostrum, a fluid secreted from the mammary glands right after the birth, is very rich in protein and contains important antibodies.

Seventh to eleventh day: During this time the baby rabbits open their eyes, and their bodies grow some soft, downy fur that gives a first hint of the later coat color and markings. Because rabbit milk is so rich and nutritious, the babies grow amazingly fast, doubling their birth weight within a week. A human baby takes six months to achieve a comparable weight gain.

Second week: Depending on their rate of development, the baby rabbits now begin to clamber out of the nest. Their fur has already become impressively thick and fluffy. They make their first attempts at grooming themselves but keep losing their balance and toppling over. Inside the nest, the doe still licks them clean after every meal and eats their excreta, which serves the double purpose of stimulating digestive activity and keeping the nest clean. If

To nurse her young a doe sits up and lets the babies crawl under her belly twice a day, where they lie on their backs and suck.

the mother drums her feet in warning while the young rabbits are outside the nest or if they are frightened by a sudden noise, they make an instant dash for safety into the nest box. If they happen to be running loose in the room, they seek refuge under some piece of furniture.

Third week: The ventures outside the nest become more frequent. The

38

young rabbits are already learning to stand on their hind legs without falling over, and they start nibbling on hay and straw.

Fourth to fifth week: Now the young keep hopping after their poor mother, trying again and again to nurse. They have learned to hop onto the nest box and onto the sofa. They have become expert broken-field runners, and watching them chase each other in play provides hilarious entertainment. It is good for young rabbits to have as much exercise as possible from the earliest time on because physical exertion helps strengthen heart, lungs, and muscles. Also, the personality and sensory capacities of rabbits raised this way are entirely different from those of rabbits that grow up confined to a hutch. By now the young rabbits begin to eat grain, but they are fondest of thick rolled oats.

From the sixth week on: The stomach and intestines are now almost completely adjusted to solid food even though the young rabbits still like to nurse.

Eighth week: Now the young rabbits are big enough to move to a new home (with the exception of Angoras, which should not be separated from their mother until they are twelve weeks old).

How Often Should a Doe Have Babies?

The median size of rabbit litters is 6. Dwarf rabbits usually bear only two to four young at a time, medium and large breeds, as many as ten. A healthy doe is capable of rearing two or three litters a year, but responsible owners and breeders don't breed their does more than once or twice a year. While she is nursing her young, a doe should receive only the highest quality food, have plenty of exercise, and always have access to drinking water.

Bottle Feeding Baby Rabbits

The younger the baby rabbits that have to be bottle reared, the slimmer the chances that they will survive, for there is no adequate substitute for rich rabbit milk. If a doe doesn't have enough milk or dies after giving birth, you can try giving the young evaporated milk. Feed the babies small amounts of it at least four times a day, using a plastic syringe (without the needle!). After each feeding, massage the abdomens carefully with one finger, and keep the rabbits warm with the help of a heat lamp at 86° F (30° C). Later, from about the third week on, you can start giving them thin oatmeal gruel and carrot juice in addition to the milk.

My tip: Try to find a doe that can serve as foster mother to your baby rabbits (make inquiries at your rabbit breeder's association, for instance).

You can check if the baby rabbits are gaining enough weight by placing them on a letter scale.

English lop, Thuringian-and-white (chamois-and-white)

New Zealand red

Belgian hare

Japanese

Dalmatian rex, three-colored

In the photos:
Different rabbit breeds. The selection in sizes and colors is huge. Dwarf rabbits, small breeds, and Angoras are best suited for apartment living.

The largest and the smallest rabbit: a German checkered giant and a Polish rabbit

Dutch rabbit, havanna-and-white

Fox rabbit, havanna

Introduction to Rabbit Breeds

From Wild to Domestic Rabbit

Domestic rabbits are descended from wild European rabbits (*Orycto-lagus cuniculus*). Fossil remains show that large tracts of western Europe were at one time populated by wild rabbits, but they were driven south during the Ice Age to Spain and northwestern Africa. Their present wider distribution is largely due to the activity of humans. Sailors took wild rabbits along on their journeys and left some of them behind on the Mediterranean islands and in Italy and later in Ireland and England.

The Origin of Rabbit Breeds

The Romans raised wild rabbits and hares for meat, keeping them in open-air enclosures. The first tame rabbits, however, seem to have been bred primarily in French monasteries. The beginnings of selective breeding go back to the sixteenth century. In the eighteenth century we find the first longhaired rabbits. In England more interest was shown in the breeding of fancy rabbits. In the United States, the Ozark region of northern Arkansas and southern Missouri has become the center of commercial rabbit production. The fancy of keeping, breeding and exhibiting rabbits has increased enormously in the last years. In 1989 the American Rabbit Breeders Association (ARBA) had more than 35,000 adult and junior members. Today there are about 50 recognized breeds.

Overview of Breeds

If I attempted to describe all the rabbit breeds there are, I would end up with a heavy tome. The following survey of classifications will at least give you an idea of how individual breeds fit into the overall picture (see photos on pages 40 and 41).

Classification by weight

Large breeds : 11 to 15¹/₂ pounds (5–7 kg) and over
Medium breeds: 7¹/₂ to 12 pounds (3.5–5.5 kg)
Small breeds: 4¹/₂ to 7¹/₂ pounds (2–3.5 kg)
Dwarf breeds: 2 to 3 pounds (1–1.5 kg)

Classification by hair length

Normal (about an inch long): most breeds (original strain); for example, New Zealand, tan and Netherlands dwarf.

Shorthairs (about ⁵/₈ of an inch long): all rex rabbits

Satin fur (like the shorthairs in length): an all-American mutation for fur rabbits; for example, black, blue, Californian, red, chinchilla, chocolate, copper and ivory.

Longhairs: Angoras and fox rabbits

Other characteristics

Upright ears: almost all rabbits
Drooping ears: lops
Fur color: white or solid-color coat
Fur with markings: for example, Dutch, checkered, English spot, Thuringian, silver marten.

What Is a Breed Standard?

Rabbit associations judge purebred rabbits at exhibitions in accordance wih a so-called standard. Similar standards are drawn up by breeders' associations for purebred cats and dogs.

Seven points that are important:
1. Weight

The tattoos in its ears tell you exactly where a purebred rabbit came from. Rabbits should be tattoed after weaning. British fanciers use rings rather than tattoos.

42

A Few Breeds at a Glance

Classification by weight:

Large breeds	Medium breeds	Small breeds	Dwarf breeds
Giants 13 to over 15 pounds (6–7 kg)	English lops 7.5 to 12 pounds (3.5–5.5 kg)	Himalayans 4.5 to 6 pounds (2–2.75 kg)	Dwarf lops 3 to 4.5 pounds (1.5–2 kg)
American check-ered giants 11 to over 13 pounds	Blue Viennese 7.5 to 11.5 pounds (3.5–5.25 kg)	Black-and-tans 5 to 7 pounds (2.25–3.25 kg)	Dwarf rabbits 2 to 3 pounds (.9–1.5 kg)
Lops 11 to over 13 pounds (5–6 kg)	Red New Zealands 7.5 to 11 pounds (3.5–5 kg)	Small chinchillas 5.5 to 7 pounds (2.5–3.25 kg)	
White giants 12 to over 14 pounds (5.5–6.5 kg)	Japanese 7 to 10 pounds (3.25–4.5 kg)	Dutch 5 to 7 pounds (2.25–3.25 kg)	

Classification by hair length and type:
(most breeds have normal-length hair)

Shorthaired breeds:	Castor rex 6.5 to 10 pounds (3–4.5 kg)		
Longhaired breeds:	Angoras 6.5 to 10 pounds (3–4.5 kg)		
	Fox rabbit 5.5 to 9 pounds (2.5–4 kg)		Dwarf fox 2 to 3 pounds (.9–1.5 kg)

Classification by ear length:

Giants ideally over 7.5 inches (19 cm)	Belgian hare 5.25 to 5.75 inches (13.5–14.5 cm)	Dutch 3.5 to 4 inches (9–10 cm)	Dwarf rabbits up to 2 inches (5.5 cm), ideally even shorter

J ust as in dogs and cats, various breeds of rabbits have specific personalities. Belgian hares and tans have a lively temperament, lops tend to be stubborn, and Angoras are the gentlest, most quiet, and most affectionate of all rabbits.

They look just like toy animals come alive —

2. Body shape and build

3. Breed type, that is, traits like texture of fur and shape of ears

4. Quality of fur

5. Breed characteristics, such as markings

6. Breed characteristics, such as color of undercoat

7. Condition

In competitions, judges award each rabbit a number of points on a scale of 0 to 100. Angora rabbits are the only breed for which an extra criterion is taken into account by the judges— namely annual production of wool.

Numbers and abbreviations you may encounter in exhibition catalogs or in ads in specialized magazines: 1,0 means one buck; 0,1 means one doe; 1,2 means one buck and two does; and so on. For additional animals of undetermined sex, a third figure may be added; for example, 2,2,3 means two bucks, two does, and three animals of undetermined sex, and 0,0,2 simply means two animals of undetermined

Three-and-a-half-week-old dwarf Angoras.

sex. When written on show cards, breeds and varieties often are abbreviated to simplify matters. The name of the breed usually is initialed in capitals, for example, A = Angora; FG = Flemish giant rNZ = Red New Zealand.

Tattoos: Purebred rabbits have tattoo marks on their ears. In the United States (where the regulations of the American Rabbit Breeders Association apply), and also in Belgium, Germany and the Netherlands, the owner's identification number or mark goes on the left ear and the registration number on the right. The British Rabbit Council uses a registration ring on a rabbit's hind leg for identification at shows. Each ring is embossed with the initials BRC, as well as the year that the ring was issued, and a letter to signify the group of breeds for which the ring should be used. Rabbits should be tatooed after weaning age.

In the photos:
A rare new breed. This new dwarf Angora is called Jamora. One (left) has zebra coloring; the other the (right) has Japanese coloring.

45

Understanding Rabbits

The social life in a rabbit colony is based on the rank order the males establish. The highest-ranking buck has to defend his position in the hierarchy every so often against males from outside the colony as well as against challengers from within the group.

Scientific Classification

It comes as a surprise to most lay-persons that rabbits, which are un-doubtedly gnawing animals, are not included in the order of rodents. As late as the end of the last century they were in fact considered part of the order *Rodentia*, but in 1912 the *Leporidae* family, which includes the European rabbit (*Oryctolagus cuniculus*), the cottontail rabbits (*Sylvilagus*), as well as hares (*Lepus*) were assigned to a new order called *Lagomorpha*. Since then scientists have found that in some respects, such as the composition of the blood serum, lagomorphs are closer to ungulates than to rodents. Anybody who is familiar with both rodents and la-gomorphs or who observes them closely will notice a number of signifi-cant differences between them: Rodents use their front limbs for grasping, which lagomorphs are unable to do. On the other hand, rabbits and hares have a habit of stretching like cats, which is something not seen in rodents.

Rabbits and Hares Are Not the Same

Most people make little distinction between rabbits and hares, a confusion that is compounded by some of the animals' vernacular names. We speak, for instance of jackrabbits, although they are really hares. Yet rabbits and hares look identical only at first glance and have very little in common beyond their taste for carrots and young greens and a habit of running in zigzag fashion, a skill both have developed to high perfection.

Why Rabbits Have Changed So Little

There is hardly another domestic animal that has retained as much of its ancestors' wild character as our rabbits. Sometimes it seems to me nothing short of a miracle that in spite of the most "unnatural" conditions we humans impose on them, these small creatures still somehow muster the strength to hold on to some of their original behavior.

Just think of the thousands and millions of rabbits that pass through our laboratories, not just to benefit science and medicine, but also to test cosmet-ics, cleansers, and laundry soaps. Or think of the Angora rabbits that are kept by the thousands on metal grates in batteries of cages primarily in the East Bloc and in China to produce fancy wool as cheaply as possible until their dying breath. And let us not forget the many outrageous breeding experiments that are practiced: ears that are so long that the animals trip on them; breeds that are judged by their weight, the heavier the better. Whether or not these poor animals are still able to hop or run is of no interest to the breeders.

Through all their tribulations, rabbits have remained patient, gentle, and silent but have retained their vitality, their courage, and an indomitable will to live. Knowing all this, you as an owner and friend of animals will want to give your rabbit a chance to develop its

Differences between Wild Hares and Rabbits at a Glance

Common hare
Lepus europaeus

Large and slender; a long-legged runner that prefers open fields.

Ears longer than the head. Solitary; seeks the company of others of its kind only during mating season.

Makes a nest and places its young in a hollow in the open country.

The youngs are born fully haired with eyes that open and ears that hear.

European wild rabbit
Oryctolagus cuniculus

Ears shorter than the head. Very gregarious; lives together with others in colonies.

Digs complex warrens where it hides from enemies and rears its young.

The young are helpless at birth, naked, blind, and deaf.

Small and rather squat but muscular; an agile sprinter and expert digger that prefers areas with soft (sandy) soil and protective shrubbery.

Gestation: about 42 days
Size of litters: 1–4 young

Chromosomes: 46

Gestation: about 31 days
Size of litter: 4–6 young

Chromosomes: 44

Meat: dark red
Weight: about 4¹/₂ to 13 pounds
(2–6 kg)
average: 9 pounds (4 kg)

Meat: light pink
Weight: about 2 to 4¹/₂ pounds
(1–2 kg)

In the photos:
Strategy for survival. Rabbits have few defenses. In order to stay alive in nature, they try to protect themselves against all kinds of enemies and dangers by developing extreme alertness combined with shyness.

Rabbits rise up on their haunches in the tall grass to get a better view of things.

natural talents to the fullest. In return, your tame little companion will "tell" you how its ancestors once lived and how its relatives in the wild still live today.

The Safety of Underground Warrens

Unlike hares, wild rabbits build complex underground warrens to which they can retreat from their enemies and where they rear their young. These warrens are the primary scene of a group's social interaction. Rabbits are decidedly territorial animals and develop a strict rank order. Thus every colony (composed of 8 to 15 members) has a dominant male and a top-ranking female acting like king and queen. Only the queen may rear her young inside the warren; lower ranking females have to dig burrows at some remove. Rabbits are peaceful animals that get into fights only rarely, as when, for instance:
• a pregnant doe defends her burrow against another female;
• young bucks act up; or
• unfamilar rabbits try to invade the colony's territory.

In these situations, rabbits, which are generally such gentle creatures, are capable of biting and scratching quite viciously.

Rabbits are extremely adaptable and, since they thrive in the vicinity of human settlements, move even into cities. There they live in parks, along railroad beds, in drainage pipes, on empty lots and sports fields, and under wood piles and barracks. But wherever they settle they need the safety and protection of burrows and other hiding places, as well as the sociability provided by other members of the tribe.

Therefore: Never introduce a new rabbit without proper precautions (see page 18) into a group that has grown into a cohesive social whole. Always provide enough nest boxes. There your rabbits will feel as safe as they would in a burrow.

Grooming is important.

Watch out, an enemy is approaching!

Odoriferous Calling Cards

Rabbits have two glands with the help of which they can leave scent marks. One is located underneath the tongue and secretes odors we humans cannot perceive (pheromones) through several pores on the underside of the chin. The other scent gland is located at the anus.

Rubbing the chin against objects: When a rabbit does this it is marking its territory and announcing to all its fellows: This is where I live. This territory is mine! In nature, wild rabbits mark stones, twigs, striking features of the landscape, and the entrances to their warrens. Pet rabbits mark chair and table legs, their cage, their food dish, and their nest box. Within its marked territory, a rabbit feels safe and at home. An area that is unmarked or marked by strange rabbits makes a rabbit feel insecure. Dominant males and females do most of the marking.

Anal marking: Through their anal glands, rabbits are able to add at will a

This rabbit is rubbing its chin up against things to mark territory. The scent rabbits leave behind is imperceptible to humans.

secretion to their droppings and thus to leave behind "chemical name plates" and calling cards. Scientists have discovered that individual rabbits not only recognize other members of the colony by their common, familiar scent but can also tell from the droppings where the other rabbit is coming from, how old it is, and what sex it is. However, wild rabbits can recognize only a limited number of their species in this way. A buck also sprays his chosen female with urine, thus marking her as belonging to him.

Why Rabbits Should Not Be Called Cowards

Rabbits are hunted by a host of predators: humans, dogs, cats, wild animals, and even birds; and they deal with their predicament by running as fast as they can. Are they cowards? It is true that in nature they are timid and easily terrified and always try to escape or hide from potential enemies. If they didn't, they would inevitably fall prey to their predators. Rabbits are consummate practitioners of nonviolence, and they manage to survive only because of their enormous adaptability, their agility, and their timidity. To put it in a nutshell—their fearfulness saves their lives.

It is true that if a rabbit is dragged from its burrow by a ferret or if it is caught in a hunter's snare, it may die hours later from sheer shock, that is, from a terror that refuses to pass. Still, rabbits are capable of courage in spite of their fearful nature. For rabbits and hares don't always run. I once witnessed, when I was out walking, how a hare made a dash for a crow, attacked it, and drove it away. Presumably the crow had tried to help itself to one of the helpless babies the mother hare had placed in a hollow in the ground on the open field. My dwarf rabbit Mümmi also diplayed a courage born of desperation one time when a huge Saint Bernard suddenly turned up near her nest box. The tiny doe launched herself at the approaching monster like a fury and bit its nose. Mümmi had no way of knowing that Bernie was nothing more than a good-natured canine pet whose only crime was curiosity. Under other circumstances, Mümmi's prospects of winning a battle with such a contestant would have been nil. As it was, the dog was startled, drew back, and ran to its mistress for consolation.

Rabbit Language—Body Language

If you want to understand your rabbit better you have to learn its body language, for rabbits hardly ever utter sounds, and if they do, the sounds are usually almost inaudible.

Stamping or drumming with the hind feet: This is an expression of fear, a threatening gesture, or a warning. Wild rabbits drum the ground loudly with their hind legs at the approach of an enemy, thus warning their fellows, which then disappear into their burrows with the speed of lightning.

Watch out! This rabbit is about to bite. If a rabbit folds its ears back, extends its head forward and its tail straight out back, you had better not touch it.

Lying flat on the ground with ears folded flat: This posture, in which a rabbit hopes to become invisible, is assumed at the sudden appearance of danger or in response to unexpected, loud noises. But watch out if your rabbit assumes this posture indoors. It may break into panicked flight and run straight into a wall.

Rising up on the haunches: A rabbit not only gets a better view of its surroundings in this posture; it also can sniff out scent sources better, see behind visual obstacles (as in tall grass), and hear better. Rabbits also rise up on their hind legs to reach tempting food, such as tender young shoots on branches. A rabbit in a cage will rise up or jump up happily when it sees its caretaker approach with food.

Rolling on the ground: This is an expression of well-being.

Relaxed squatting with ears folded back: This is a resting posture.

Sometimes rabbits also move their jaws contentedly, as though chewing. Don't disturb your rabbit when it is in this mood.

Lying on the side with one leg outstretched and eyes falling shut: The animal wants to go to sleep. Rabbits often lie down like this when they are exhausted. Sometimes, if they are too hot or have been running hard, they stretch out both hind legs.

Light nudging with the nose: Sometimes this is merely a gesture of greeting, but it can also be a request to be petted.

Forceful pushing away of the hand: The rabbit is telling you that it has had enough petting.

Brief shaking of the ears: I have observed this behavior mostly in larger breeds with long ears. It means "That's enough!" Rabbits do it after being brushed and shorn or if they have been held too long.

Licking of the hand: This means "Thank you" or "I like you." Sometimes, once they have started licking while being petted, they get carried away and go on to lick the floor after you have withdrawn your hand. Rabbits also express affection toward each other by mutual licking.

Tense body, straight tail, head stretched forward, ears pointing straight ahead: This posture ex-

Rabbits seeking cover from danger flatten themselves against the ground and fold their ears as close to the body as possible. You will see this instinctive reaction in your indoor pet rabbit, too.

The glands that secrete the scents used by rabbits to mark their territory are much larger in male animals than in females. A buck with an especially "productive" scent gland generally is accepted as dominant.

51

This dark hole looks intriguing.

Let's see what's inside.

presses concentration, curiosity, and, at the same time, caution. Rabbits meeting for the first time assume this stance before sniffing each other. Watch out: If the rabbit now folds its ears back, the mood has turned aggressive. Attack and biting may follow.

Rubbing the chin against things (see page 49): The rabbit is marking the objects with a substance, odorless to humans, which is produced by a scent gland under the tongue and secreted through pores underneath the chin. It is a rabbit's way of marking territory and announcing to its fellows: "This belongs to me."

Ingesting fecal matter (see page 20): The feces are usually taken directly from the anus. They are special excretions from the cecum— moist, glistening, and kidney-shaped—

not round and dry like normal rabbit droppings. These special feces are an important source of vitamin B. Ingesting them is totally different from coprophagy, that is, eating of dung, and there is nothing disgusting about it.

Digging and scratching: The rabbit is trying to construct a burrow. This behavior is very pronounced in does that are in heat or pregnant. But sometimes digging simply indicates a desire for physical affection, "Keep on petting me!" My doe Mohrle also scratches in her litter box when she detects an unfamilar smell there of which she doesn't approve. Excited bucks also scratch the ground, for instance at the approach of a rival.

Sound Utterances

Rabbits are very quiet animals, but they are by no means mute. However,

Pretty long, this pipe.

Here I am again.

you have to listen very closely in order to hear them.

Muttering: Short scolding noises uttered in quick succession. A rabbit

Rabbits usually pick up the vitamin-rich excretions of the cecum directly from the anus. Ingestion of this substance is crucial for their health and has nothing in common with the unappetizing habit of eating regular feces.

that mutters like this is either angry or expressing some warning. A pregnant doe will issue such a warning if an insistent buck refuses to leave her in peace.

Hissing: Hissing is always aggressive in intent, and a short hiss may precede an attack. The hissing of rabbits has little in common with the hissing of cats.

A short muttering or growling sound: This is mostly heard from a buck shortly after the act of mating.

Soft or loud squeaking: Baby rabbits sometimes squeak when they are afraid or hungry. I was once awakened at night by such a squeak for help when a doe had deposited a newly born baby rabbit next to my bed. Luckily I was able to return the shivering little creature in time to the warm nest with its siblings.

In contrast to the normal, round feces (right), the excretions of the cecum (left) are kidney-shaped, moist and shiny, and sometimes stuck together in grape-like clusters.

53

Sensory Capacities of (Wild) Rabbits

	Organ and its physical characteristics	Capacities
Sight	Large eyes placed high on the sides of the head; radius vision of each eye: 170.5 degrees	Large field of vision, which is crucial to the survival of this prey animal.
	The fields of vision of the two eyes overlap very little.	Wide, panoramic view but limited distinction of detail; poor depth perception.
	Poor adaptation to light changes; unlike in higher mammals and humans the pupils can't widen and contract.	Can't see well in bright sunlight.
	Large lenses with great capacity for light absorption.	Relatively good vision in twilight (rabbits are active at dusk).
	Eyes specialized for distance vision, as in most prey animals that rely on flight for survival.	Close up vision limited.
Hearing	Ears shaped like elongated funnels.	Immediate perception of sounds.
	Each ear can turn independently of the other.	Field of hearing is 360 degrees; the faintest sound from anywhere can be pinpointed.
Smell	The nose has 100 million scent cells; mobile nostrils.	Highly acute sense of smell; detects volatile scent molecules. Recognizes identity of rabbit that has left a scent mark.
Taste	The tongue has 8,000 taste buds; dogs, by comparison, have 48,000.	Has preferences for some foods, dislikes others; doesn't necessarily recognize poisonous substances.
Touch	Whiskers that are as long as the body is wide.	Help measure the width of the warren's passages and find the way in the dark. Tactile stimuli are also received by the entire body surface.

monocular vision 170.5° — binocular vision 10° — monocular vision 170.5°

Rabbit

binocular vision 9°
no blind spot;

monocular vision 80° — monocular vision 80°

Cat

blind spot 80°

Conclusions to be drawn for the handling of pet rabbits:

With shy rabbits that don't yet feel fully at home, be careful to move quietly and slowly; otherwise they may respond with reflex-like flight.

Rabbits can literally run between your feet because their spatial perception and close up vision are so poor.

Bright sunlight and a light suddenly turned on in a dark room are blinding to rabbits.

If you want to watch wild rabbits, stay quietly in the shade of a tree downwind from the animal. This way it will fail to notice you.

A rabbit's ears are very sensitive to noise. Slamming doors, screaming, and loud barking of a dog close by frighten rabbits and may cause flight. These loud noises should therefore be avoided.

The smell of strong household cleansers, a perfume that is too penetrating, and sometimes the scent of strangers give offense to a rabbit's delicate nose.

Don't count on your rabbit to be able to distinguish poisonous plants from harmless ones. That's something *you* have to watch out for!

Never pull the sensitive whiskers of a rabbit, nor cut them off. Pet nervous or excited animals slowly and gently to soothe them. Body contact such as the sensation of being inside a protective burrow (or nest) and the presence of another rabbit, has a calming effect.

In the photos:
The daily run outside the cage. Rabbits, even if they are a mere four weeks old, enjoy surroundings that offer variety the opportunity to chase each other and hide. A sofa with lots of soft pillows is especially wonderful for jumping.

A sofa makes a wonderful playground.

Loud grinding of the teeth combined with a dull look in the eyes and general apathy: This is always a sign of terrible pain, as when a rabbit has tympanites. It should not be confused with

soft teeth-grinding sounds produced when the jaws move as in chewing, which expresses a feeling of comfort and is displayed primarily when you scratch a rabbit on the back of the neck. Some rabbits exhibit this behavior more than others.

High-pitched, piercing screams: This sound is produced only in a state of mortal terror or under excruciating pain, as when a predator grasps a rabbit and inflicts a killing bite.

Some Amazing Capacities

Wild rabbits are extremely adaptable. The following examples show how quickly they can adjust to almost any condition of the environment.

Birth control: The exact sources for this behavior are not yet known, but in certain stress situations, as during periods of acute food shortage, the physical organism of the does refuses to carry young to term. The fetuses die *in utero* and are completely reabsorbed by the doe's body. Of course the opposite—excessive fecundity—is common in rabbits, too, especially if humans introduce them into environments that lack the natural predators of rabbits. In 1859, an English settler released a dozen domestic rabbits in Australia. By 1907, Australia had a rabbit population of over 100 million. Their number kept growing until the early 1940s when it reached 750 million. It was not until Australian rabbits were deliberately exposed to myxomatosis, a deadly rabbit disease, that this frenzied reproduction was brought under some control.

Adaptability: If forced by necessity, rabbits sometimes can become adventurous in their food habits. Thus some rabbits left on the sparsely vegetated Kerguelen Islands in the southern Indian Ocean survived the raw antarctic climate there and resorted to eating Kerguelen cabbage, a plant sailors on whaling boats appreciated as a wholesome vegetable; and when this cabbage was all gone, the rabbits turned to seaweed for food. It has also been observed that rabbits, which are by nature burrowing animals, will, if they find themselves in swampy areas, build their nests in willow trees.

These various facts hopefully will give you some idea of the nature of rabbits. Understanding and enjoyment are the best foundation for developing a friendship between people and animals.

Getting up on the back . . .

. . . and down again.

Check List for Spotting Possible Health Problems and Diseases

What you notice	Possible causes you can eliminate yourself
Droppings that are soft to runny and may smell sour. Anus and abdomen soiled with feces.	Sudden change in diet (as from dry food to fresh), spoiled food, food or water that is too cold, intestinal problems caused by wet bedding or drafts.
The rabbit stops eating and produces only tiny, hard droppings or nothing at all in spite of painful straining; body may be somewhat bloated.	Too little exercise, insufficient water, abrupt change from fresh to all dry food; may be a symptom of an infectious disease or a result of eating spoiled food.
Some clear discharge from the nose, occasional sneezing.	Irritation from vapors of strong cleansers or from dusty hay; vitamin deficiency; generally weakened resistance. (There are some rabbits that are allergic to hay!)
Tearing eyes; reddened and, sometimes, swollen eyelids; discharge of pus from eyes.	Symptoms of colds; irritation caused by dust or foreign body; injury from scratching bites, or overgrown wooly hair, (in Angoras, for instance.)
Accelerated breathing, trembling body.	Overheating caused by direct exposure to the sun or proximity to a hot radiator.
Reddening of skin, minor loss of hair, small bald spots.	Shedding in the spring and fall, allergy; vitamin deficiency; fur pulled out or bitten off by another rabbit.
Sitting around apathetically, moving too little.	Loneliness; pining for a social partner; too little attention from humans; boredom; lack of interesting and stimulating places to run. (Rabbits also become more sedentary with age.)

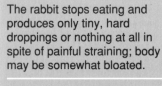

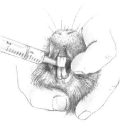

You can give your rabbit medicines by sticking a plastic syringe (without the needle) into the cheek behind the incisors. Hold the rabbit steady with a firm grip on the nape, and push the plunger of the syringe down slowly, so that the animal doesn't choke on the liquid.

Cause for alarm if combined with these symptoms	Possible diagnosis requiring immediate treatment by veterinarian
Refuses food, loses strength, sits in the cage trembling with fear, grinds teeth loudly in pain, bloated body, blood in stool.	Poisoning from chemically treated produce; intestinal infection, most commonly coccidiosis (highly contagious to other rabbits and especially dangerous for young animals); be sure to take along a stool sample; isolate the sick animal.
Strongly bloated body, loud grind- of teeth, violent drumming with the back legs; shortness of breath and impaired circulation.	Tympanites; take animal to the veterinarian immediately; may be fatal.
Thick discharge of pus from the nose, which the rabbit tries to get rid of by snorting and wiping with the paws; chest and front legs sticky with mucus. Also, loss of appetite, general weakness, and coughing.	Contagious cold (separate the animal immediately from other rabbits); beginnings of pneumonia, which often follows a cold.
Eyes swelling shut; lumps of dough- or jelly-like consistency on the head; more and more boils that erupt.	Myxomatosis, which is practically always fatal; in areas where this disease is prevalent, rabbits should be vaccinated against it.
Nostrils flaring; violently trembling body; mouth perhaps open; very fast, shallow breathing.	Heat stroke; very serious; take the animal to the veterinarian instantly; if he or she cannot be reached, see instructions for emergency treatment!
Considerable loss of hair, sticky and crusty scabs, frequent scratching; rabbit holds head at a tilt and shakes it.	Mange (mite infestation), fungi.
Rabbit no longer hops or runs; teeth grinding indicating pain; legs sometimes pulled close to body, sometimes stretched out unnaturally, sometimes dragged along behind; loss of equilibrium.	Fracture; torn ligament; a joint pulled out of its socket; internal injury from from being caught in a closing door or from being dropped; paralysis due to hereditary disease.

The upper and lower incisors should meet like this to wear properly.

Incisors that don't wear down properly curl inward like horns and interfere with food intake.

Helpful Information and Books

Information and Periodicals

The American Rabbit Breeders Association (ARBA)
1925 South Main, Box 426
Bloomington, IL 81701

The ARBA publishes a magazine devoted to the fancy: *Domestic Rabbits.* It contains much useful information on old and new breeds, supplies of stock, and equipment, as well as news about the shows that are held regularly in most parts of the country. An annual subscription is modestly priced, and there are reduced fees for children, senior citizens, and family groups.

Another monthly magazine is: *Rabbits.*
Countryside Publications, Ltd.
312 Portland Road, Highway 19 East
Waterloo, WI 53594

All serious rabbit fanciers in the United Kingdom should subscribe to the biweekly magazine *Fur and Feather*, the official magazine of the British Rabbit Council (BRC).

Fur and Feather
British Rabbit Council (BRC)
Purfoy House
7 Kirkgate
Newark
Nottingham, England

Membership in the BRC is also essential for the English rabbit enthusiast, as this is the governing body of the fancy. The annual subscription fee is small, and there are reduced rates for children, family groups, pensioners, and so on. The official series of rabbit rings supplied by the Council to members helps them maintain records of their stock.

Books

The American Rabbit Breeders Association, *Official Guide to Raising Better Rabbits,* Bloomington, Illinois.
——, *Standard of Perfection: Standard Bred Rabbits and Cavies,* Bloomington, Illinois.
Arrington, L.R., and Kathleen Kelley, *Domestic Rabbit Biology and Production,* University Presses of Florida, Gainesville, Florida.
Bennet, Bob, *Raising Rabbits the Modern Way,* Garden Way, Pownal, Vermont, 1988.
Downing, Elisabeth, *Keeping Rabbits,* Pelham Books, London, 1979.
Fritzsche, Helga, *Rabbits,* Barron's, Hauppauge, New York, 1983.
Harkness, John and Joseph Wagner, *The Biology and Medicine of Rabbits and Rodents,* Lea & Febiger, Philadelphia, Pennsylvania, 1988.
National Research Council, *Nutrient Requirements of Rabbits,* 2nd edition, National Academy Press, Washington, D.C., 1977.
Sandford, J.C., *The Domestic Rabbit,* Collins, London, 1986.
Vriends-Parent, Lucia, *The New Rabbit Handbook,* Barron's, Hauppage, New York, 1989.
Wegler, Monika, *Dwarf Rabbits,* Barron's, Hauppauge, New York, 1986.

Perfect for Pet Owners!

PET OWNER'S MANUALS

Over 50 illustrations per book (20 or more color photos), 72–80 pp., paperback.

AFRICAN GRAY PARROTS (3773-1)
AMAZON PARROTS (4035-X)
BANTAMS (3687-5)
BEAGLES (3829-0)
BEEKEEPING (4089-9)
BOSTON TERRIERS (1696-3)
BOXERS (4036-8)
CANARIES (4611-0)
CATS (4442-8)
CHINCHILLAS (4037-6)
CHOW-CHOWS (3952-1)
CICHLIDS (4597-1)
COCKATIELS (4610-2)
COCKER SPANIELS (1478-2)
COCKATOOS (4159-3)
COLLIES (1875-3)
CONURES (4880-6)
DACHSHUNDS (1843-5)
DALMATIANS (4605-6)
DISCUS FISH (4669-2)
DOBERMAN PINSCHERS (2999-2)
DOGS (4822-9)
DOVES (1855-9)
DWARF RABBITS (1352-2)
ENGLISH SPRINGER SPANIELS (1778-1)
FEEDING AND SHELTERING BACKYARD
  BIRDS (4252-2)
FEEDING AND SHELTERING EUROPEAN
  BIRDS (2858-9)
FERRETS (2976-3)
GERBILS (3725-1)
GERMAN SHEPHERDS (2982-8)
GOLDEN RETRIEVERS (3793-6)
GOLDFISH (2975-5)
GOULDIAN FINCHES (4523-8)
GREAT DANES (1418-9)
GUINEA PIGS (4612-9)
GUPPIES, MOLLIES, AND PLATTIES (1497-9)
HAMSTERS (4439-8)
IRISH SETTERS (4663-3)
KEESHONDEN (1560-6)
KILLIFISH (4475-4)
LABRADOR RETRIEVERS (3792-8)
LHASA APSOS (3950-5)
LIZARDS IN THE TERRARIUM (3925-4)
LONGHAIRED CATS (2803-1)
LONG-TAILED PARAKEETS (1351-4)

LORIES AND LORIKEETS (1567-3)
LOVEBIRDS (3726-X)
MACAWS (4768-0)
MICE (2921-6)
MUTTS (4126-7)
MYNAHS (3688-3)
PARAKEETS (4437-1)
PARROTS (4823-7)
PERSIAN CATS (4405-3)
PIGEONS (4044-9)
POMERANIANS (4670-6)
PONIES (2856-2)
POODLES (2812-0)
POT BELLIES AND OTHER MINIATURE PIGS
  (1356-5)
PUGS (1824-9)
RABBITS (4440-1)
RATS (4535-1)
ROTTWEILERS (4483-5)
SCHNAUZERS (3949-1)
SCOTTISH FOLD CATS (4999-3)
SHAR-PEI (4334-2)
SHEEP (4091-0)
SHETLAND SHEEPDOGS (4264-6)
SHIH TZUS (4524-6)
SIAMESE CATS (4764-8)
SIBERIAN HUSKIES (4265-4)
SMALL DOGS (1951-2)
SNAKES (2813-9)
SPANIELS (2424-9)
TROPICAL FISH (4700-1)
TURTLES (4702-8)
WEST HIGHLAND WHITE TERRIERS (1950-4)
YORKSHIRE TERRIERS (4406-1)
ZEBRA FINCHES (3497-X)

NEW PET HANDBOOKS

Detailed, illustrated profiles (40–60 color photos), 144 pp., paperback.

NEW AQUARIUM FISH HANDBOOK (3682-4)
NEW AUSTRALIAN PARAKEET
  HANDBOOK (4739-7)
NEW BIRD HANDBOOK (4157-7)
NEW CANARY HANDBOOK (4879-2)
NEW CAT HANDBOOK (2922-4)
NEW COCKATIEL HANDBOOK (4201-8)
NEW DOG HANDBOOK (2857-0)
NEW DUCK HANDBOOK (4088-0)
NEW FINCH HANDBOOK (2859-7)
NEW GOAT HANDBOOK (4090-2)

NEW PARAKEET HANDBOOK (2985-2)
NEW PARROT HANDBOOK (3729-4)
NEW RABBIT HANDBOOK (4202-6)
NEW SALTWATER AQUARIUM
  HANDBOOK (4482-7)
NEW SOFTBILL HANDBOOK (4075-9)
NEW TERRIER HANDBOOK (3951-3)

REFERENCE BOOKS

Comprehensive, lavishly illustrated references (60–300 color photos), 136–176 pp., hardcover & paperback.

AQUARIUM FISH (1350-6)
AQUARIUM FISH BREEDING (4474-6)
AQUARIUM FISH SURVIVAL MANUAL
  (5686-8)
AQUARIUM PLANTS MANUAL (1687-4)
BEFORE YOU BUY THAT PUPPY (1750-1)
BEST PET NAME BOOK EVER, THE
  (4258-1)
CARING FOR YOUR SICK CAT (1726-9)
CAT CARE MANUAL (5765-1)
CIVILIZING YOUR PUPPY (4953-5)
COMMUNICATING WITH YOUR DOG
  (4203-4)
COMPLETE BOOK OF BUDGERIGARS
  (6059-8)
COMPLETE BOOK OF CAT CARE (4613-7)
COMPLETE BOOK OF DOG CARE (4158-5)
COMPLETE BOOK OF PARROTS (5971-9)
DOG CARE MANUAL (5764-3)
FEEDING YOUR PET BIRD (1521-3)
GOLDFISH AND ORNAMENTAL CARP
  (9286-4)
GUIDE TO A WELL BEHAVED CAT
  (1476-6)
GUIDE TO HOME PET GROOMING
  (4298-0)
HEALTHY DOG, HAPPY DOG (1842-7)
HOP TO IT: A Guide to Training Your Pet Rabbit
  (4551-3)
HORSE CARE MANUAL (1133-3)
HOW TO TALK TO YOUR CAT (1749-8)
HOW TO TEACH YOUR OLD DOG
  NEW TRICKS (4544-0)
LABYRINTH FISH (5635-3)
MACAWS (9037-3)
NONVENOMOUS SNAKES (5632-9)
WATER PLANTS IN THE AQUARIUM (3926-2)

Barron's Educational Series, Inc. • 250 Wireless Blvd., Hauppauge, NY 11788
Call toll-free: 1-800-645-3476 • In Canada: Georgetown Book Warehouse
34 Armstrong Ave., Georgetown, Ont. L7G 4R9 • Call toll-free: 1-800-247-7160
ISBN prefix: 0-8120 • Order from your favorite book or pet store

BARRON'S

R 6/94

Index

Bold face indicates color photos. C1 indicates front cover; C2, inside front cover; C3, inside back cover; C4, back cover.

Note of Warning

This book deals with the care of pet rabbits. It is possible to get scratched or bitten when handling a pet rabbit. If this happens, have a doctor treat the injuries immediately.

Gnawing on things is part of natural rabbit behavior. You therefore have to supervise your rabbit during its important daily period of running free in the apartment. Be especially careful to keep your rabbit from chewing on electric wires, which can have fatal consequences.

Some people have allergic reactions to rabbit hair. If you think you might be allergic, consult your doctor before getting a rabbit.

The Photos on the Covers
Front Cover: Six-week-old domestic rabbit
Inside front cover: A yellow-and-white lop, a black-and-tan dwarf rabbit, an Angora rabbit, and a checkered rabbit (from left to right).
Inside back cover: Six-week-old blue-and-white dwarf rabbit.
Back cover: A recently shorn yellow Angora rabbit and a mongrel are helping themselves to a snack.
Photographer: Monika Wegler.

English translation © Copyright 1990
by Barron's Educational Series, Inc.

© Copyright 1989 by Gräfe and Unzer
GmbH, Munich, West Germany
The title of the German book is *Kaninchen*

Translated from the German by Rita and Robert
Kimber

All inquiries should be addressed to:
Barron's Educational Series, Inc.
250 Wireless Boulevard
Hauppauge, NY 11788

Library of Congress Catalog Card No. 90-30129

International Standard Book No. 0-8120-4440-1

Library of Congress Cataloging-in-Publication Data
Wegler, Monika.
[Kaninchen. English]
Rabbits: how to take care of them and understand them / by Monika Wegler; with color photographs by Monika Wegler and drawings by György Jankovics.
p. cm.
Translation of: Kaninchen.
ISBN 0-8120-4440-1
1. Rabbits. I. Jankovics, György. II. Title.
SF453.W4413   1990
636'.9322—dc20   90-30129
                                          CIP

PRINTED AND BOUND IN HONG KONG

456   9927   9